The Eye of the Dragon

Stalking Castaneda

6/29/2012

Also by S. Guzman-C.

A Vagabond in Mexico

The Eye of the Dragon
Stalking Castaneda

S. Guzman-C

Nomads Press

Published by
Nomads Press
5694 Mission Center Road 602 Ste. 216
San Diego, CA 92108

Cover art by the author

First Edition 2011
10 9 8 7 6 5 4 3 2 1

Library of Congress Catalog Card Number: 2011912668
ISBN: 9781461115922

The events in this story indeed happened; therefore, to protect the people's privacy, names have been changed, altered
or omitted altogether.

For the spirit of humanity.

Contents

Mind nor intellect, nor ego, feeling;
Sky nor earth nor metals am I
I am It*, I am It, Blessed Spirit, I am It!
No birth, no death, no caste have I:
Father, mother, have I none.
I am It, I am It, Blessed Spirit, I am It!
Beyond the flights of fancy, formless am I,
Permeating the limbs of all life;
Bondage I do not fear; I am free, ever free,
I am It, I am It, Blessed Spirit, I am It!
                                    —Lord Shankara

---

* "It" substitutes "He" in this version.

We do not receive wisdom, we must discover it for ourselves, after a journey through the wilderness, which no one can make for us.
—Marcel Proust

Wouldn't take nothing for my journey now.—Maya Angelou

Only by becoming invisible, and then nothing, can we pass through the eye of the dragon.   —Chinese mythology

Preface

When the Guru fails what happens depends on each disciple's merits. —Sri Ramana Maharshi

In days long past (not fully aware of what I was doing, I must confess), I left everything behind in search of the eye of the dragon. At the beginning of my journey, I came across the teachings of don Juan, a Yaqui Indian shaman, through the books of Carlos Castaneda. Don Juan's ancient Toltec[*] wisdom was a beacon, but in the year 2001, I came across critical information, which proved conclusively that many of Castaneda's claims were fraudulent.

At the time, I had verified much of what he had written about, and the new and discrediting facts greatly puzzled me. They also forced me to question my findings and convictions, and to look in other directions to take new bearings.

Furthermore, it had been claimed that Castaneda had left this world in full consciousness taking his body with him. And the turmoil that Castaneda's ordinary death (due to cancer of the liver) caused in many of his closest followers, made me realize how blind human beings can be, and how ready we are to miss a point and become either judges or victims.

---

[*] The Nahuatl word "Toltec" actually means "craftsman of the highest level," and, in this book, refers to a lineage of ancient scientists and artists, dedicated to a higher learning and a specific spiritual discipline, not to the archaeological Toltec civilization centered at Tula in Mexico.

I am writing these notes with a double purpose: To help me get a better perspective and a new direction, and to maybe help a few others do the same.

And in case you don't know Castaneda, I'll tell you a little about his work as I go along, for it was a great help in my search for the eye of the dragon. I will also juxtapose his work with other works that have also been helpful. I won't delve into any of these works; that is unnecessary.

I will just say that their main and recurring theme is our destructive egomania, and I'll let my own experience illustrate. It behooves you to do your own research, and confirm the damaging effects of an unchecked ego, for being the bane of humanity its study is worthy of our consideration.

Consider this: In an article I once came across in a monthly magazine, I read about a six-year-old boy who died after breaking his neck under an extremely heavy load, too heavy for the child to carry. The article also said that he had been a slave all his life.

The author knew this because archeologists are trained to read bones. And the child's bones, together with other bones (a mass grave for slaves), had been found while excavating somewhere in New York City (of all places) to lay the foundations for a new building.

His bones not only told this archeologist how he had died but also how he had lived. They told him that he had been overworked all his life, that he had been malnourished, that he probably never had a loving arm around him. Those bones finally told the archeologist that that unbearable load had killed him at the tender age of six years old.

Should I ever feel sorry for myself? But perhaps a more pertinent question would be, should I ever feel sorry for that little boy? For just like that little boy I am going to die, and although longer, my life might well end up being much more miserable than his was.

For only by reducing my self-importance to the lowest, can I claim to be different from his captors and murderers; there is such a thing as collective responsibility, a social contract. We all endorse a social contract that thrives in egomania, an egomania that causes the suffering of humanity by rendering us blind to the Whole.

Carlos Castaneda is dead, but his controversial legacy remains.

Introduction

Man is unhappy because he doesn't know he is happy. It's only that. That's all, that's all! If anyone finds out, he'll become happy at once, that minute.   —Fyodor Dostoyevsky

The *intent* behind Castaneda's shamanic books, is to help us become warriors who conquer ourselves; warriors who develop an awareness of our full potential as human beings. Apprentices are grouped as *dreamers* or *stalkers,* in an effort to classify them according to their abilities and energy configuration, but in fact, they have to be both; *stalking* helps *dreaming* and vice versa.

Stalking is the art of developing a strategy to deal with the world as a spiritual warrior; *dreaming* is the art of controlling your dreams to develop your *other* self, the *dreaming body.* *Stalking* also helps when fixing the new position of the assemblage point while *dreaming.*

According to Castaneda, dreams occur due to the movement of an *assemblage point—the point where perception is assembled.** This point (located at arm's length behind us, between the shoulder blades) supposedly moves naturally while we sleep, changing our perception. If we volitionally hold that

---

* Sri Ramana Maharshi, called by some the greatest sage of the twentieth century, says that the Self (Spirit) resides in the body in a point located to the right side of the chest, but that that *point* is only a way to make something incomprehensible at least referable; for everything is in the Self. If we are in the Self, 'It' can't really be contained in us. Although Maharshi is from India, he affirms (like the Buddha) that there is no reincarnation.

new position while we dream we are also *stalking* that dream and doing *dreaming*—the same thing we unwittingly do with this *dream* called life. Some call this process of controlling a dream *lucid dreaming*.

In Castaneda's world I was a *dreamer*. And the *dreaming* experience that I am about to relate in the following paragraphs is an example of a *dreaming* technique that I arrived at after years of practice, please follow me.

I could hear the branches overhanging my porch, rustling in the cool summer breeze. My neighbors were away that night, and not a sound came from their apartment. I lay on my back, closed my eyes, and, after overcoming the barrage of meaningless random thoughts, my mind drifted into silence. Keeping my eyes closed, I looked for the color orange. Soon an orange circle appeared; it expanded into nothing, appearing again to expand once more and once more and once more . . .

Suddenly, a scene appeared! In front of me I was *seeing* a building and a road; the long brick building had an architectural design that I had never seen before. I was sure that the vision would soon vanish due to my inability to hold it, as was usually the case. But to my surprise, the scene stayed. I decided to hold it for as long as I could in an effort to train (using Castaneda's terminology) my *dreaming attention*.

Soon, it startled me to realize that the building and the rutted dirt road in front of me were staying. I also understood that I could enter another world through that vision, a world perhaps as *real* as my day-to-day *reality*.

As soon as the realization struck me, I felt myself being pulled into the vision. *I* (or my *dreaming body*) was no longer lying on my cot, but standing inside the covered bed of a two-and-a-half ton truck. I climbed down while disentangling my pants, which had stuck somewhere—probably a trick of my mind to distract me, since our reason will always feel threatened when unable to explain an event. I surveyed my surroundings.

It was obvious that I was not in the United States. I was nowhere that I could recognize. I meandered down the dirt road trying to figure out where I was. It seemed hot, maybe tropical. I saw a group of teenagers, stripped to the waist, tobogganing down the slope of a dirt hill on pieces of cardboard. I approached them.

"Where am I?" After I asked, I realized that the young man to whom I had addressed the question seemed to be mentally retarded, or perhaps he suffered a speech impediment of some sort, but his closest companion answered:

"Morocco!"

"Morocco," I thought.

After thanking them, I continued my stroll. I wanted to verify that my *dreaming* experience was really taking place in Morocco; it is seldom that I can verify where I have been when *dreaming*. The places that I visit seem to be usually phantom worlds of my own making.

It was a bright, sunny day. It seemed that I was close to the ocean, but I couldn't see it. I did see some black men dressed in white tunics, wearing yarmulkes. I strolled uphill toward the park, where they were chatting around a long wooden bench sans a backrest.

As I approached them, I surveyed my surroundings again. The park ahead had grass that seemed to have been recently mowed. I don't remember any trees, although I saw long winding walkways and extensive terrain. I stopped briefly and looked back to make sure that I could retrace my steps to the truck, as if there was an entrance there to my everyday world. But I didn't need an entrance; shortly after I continued my stroll, I found myself back in my apartment.

I was baffled. Never before had I entered the *dreaming attention* but in sleep. This was a new and unexpected development. I figured that I had gone somewhere, Morocco? And it had happened while I was awake; I had entered that vision, that *somewhere,* awake!

Next morning, I looked for Morocco in the World Wide Web, and there they were—the long brick buildings! And people were wearing long white tunics and yarmulkes. I couldn't be certain, of course, maybe the place I visited wasn't Morocco. But that was irrelevant. The relevant new development was that I had entered that world, with my *dreaming body,* while fully awake. That meant to me that by merely stilling my mind, I had been able to hold a vision (*stalk* it) and enter *dreaming* with my *other* self.

Hitherto, I had always entered *dreaming* by looking at my hands while having a common dream. According to Castaneda, the volitional act of looking at your hands (or whatever) gives you control of the dream; and from then on it becomes *dreaming,* a controlled experience as linear and real as your everyday life but without the physical body, so nothing limits your movements. *Dreaming* is a door to the *second attention*; it is also a way to the *third attention*, to Infinity. The *dreaming body* becomes the *other.*[†]

The *dreaming* experience mentioned before was indeed a new development for me, and it opened doors that I didn't know existed; it gave me a new perspective. This happened for the first time some fifteen years ago. Since then, however, new findings have altered that new perspective. I have come to realize that *dreaming,* or any other psychic power that we may develop, don't have much to do with awakening; in fact, it could be a help but also a hindrance.

This *dream* is for us to enjoy. The path to inner knowledge seems to be a difficult winding road because of our own mindset. To follow that path has been compared by ancient sages to walking the edge of a razor, because of our destructive self-absorption, which clouds our vision and turns our *dream* into a nightmare, or into sheer hell. In truth, everything is handed to us. Or, to paraphrase the Christ, although we do not see it, the kingdom of heaven is spread out upon the earth.

But let me start from the beginning.

[†] Tenzin Wangyal Rinpoche, a Lama in the Bon-Buddhism tradition of Tibet, explains in his writings that awareness of the present moment in our everyday life, leads to awareness and volition in dreams (the development of the *dreaming body*). The *dreaming body* he explains can meet teachers and mentors from other ages and realms. Our awareness in *dreams* can also lead us to awareness at the time of death, so that we can find our freedom. The Lama is the author of *The Tibetan Yogas of Dream and Sleep,* in which he explains different techniques to help you develop the *dreaming* volition and your daily awareness.

Chapter 1
Erasing Personal History

For me the world is weird because it is stupendous, awesome, mysterious, unfathomable; my interest has been to convince you that you must assume responsibility for being here in this marvelous world, in this marvelous desert, at this marvelous time.
—Don Juan, *Journey to Ixtlan*

The revolutionary '60s were just past, and the civil rights movement had begun in earnest. It was a period of transformation. Change was in the air, or so it seemed.

It was during this period in time that I came across a book that was to have a great influence in me; it ushered in a journey of discovery that would make me fully aware of the human predicament. The book was titled *Journey to Ixtlan* by Carlos Castaneda.

The book was just there, lying on the living room table at my mother's house; it was there in the nick of time. I was ready. I had extensive preparation. I could understand perfectly well the need to get rid of my self importance, erase personal history and take responsibility for my acts. I could see clearly how encumbering were the expectations of the people who thought that they knew me well. So I decided, as a first step, to drop my personal history.

I didn't change my name nor did anything drastic. I just started erasing my personal history by not reinforcing it anymore, and by changing my surroundings. Nobody knows who I am with certainty anymore, not even myself. It was a first step to reduce an overwhelming ego and to dismantle the conditioned mind.

The decision to leave my homeland behind for good was well thought and final. I was hearing the beat of a different drummer. I was beginning to change my direction, leaving behind a corporate world for which I was losing respect.

I had arrived at the disturbing conclusion that something was askew in the way human beings interact and perceive life. I wondered what it was that I knew that I didn't know that I knew.

In addition, perhaps due to my apparent erratic behavior, my girlfriend had recently dumped me. Nothing was holding me there.

o o o

As an immediate result of such an action, I found myself completely on my own. In many ways, I was *putting my life on the line*. Thus, I was unwittingly using three of the seven principles of the *art of stalking*, which Castaneda taught years later, for I was also *leaving everything behind* to *choose my battleground*. Eventually, I would cut all my connections.

On the surface, it was a journey taken due to personal reasons. On the surface, it seemed, and I believed myself, that I was looking for new circumstances. But the fact is that we all have a journey that we must embark on; we can refuse that journey only to our own detriment. In my case, the road itself would determine my fate; it would help me to fully understand that I had embarked on a journey of exploration with no particular destination.

But, isn't it true? Only by taking the risks that we must take do we really live, and it was such an exhilarating feeling. In a spirit of adventure, I traveled throughout the United States, Mexico, Central America, South America, and Canada. I was open to what the road could bring, to whatever I could learn about this and other realities. It was my path with heart.

I never use hallucinogens; I never have. Having been a Yoga practitioner, and influenced by Herman Hesse's work, I strongly suspected that wisdom could only be acquired through hard work; hallucinogens, I saw, were unnecessary and dangerous dead-end streets. What attracted me to the Toltec's way of life was precisely the path with heart, the discipline of "the warrior's way."

o o o

Strolling at leisure through Old San Juan, I basked in mottled sunshine. It was a farewell stroll, the last time I saw the historic town or trod its cobbled streets. Suddenly, there stood Lucy, radiant.

We conversed. She told me that she was getting married soon. I wished her the best—in years past, in the follies of youth, I had let her go. Lucy looked inquiringly at me with her piercing black eyes, and I explained that I was leaving.

"I knew you'd leave," she said.

o o o

The first time I did *dreaming* I was in Hawaii.

Lo and behold! Hawaii! World famous Oahu's Waikiki Beach and the Diamond Head Volcano! The names connote beautiful, voluptuous and accessible women, young mountains with high peaks, and pristine beaches with a myriad of tourists and surfers—all true.

At the time of my visit, there were also hookers and hippies galore, and travelers like me doing odd jobs (or diving for pukka shells to make necklaces to sell) as a way to meet their traveling expenses. And I know you deserve a better description of Hawaii, but I find it so overdone that I will recommend you to read *Hawaii* by James Michener. I read it while I was living in Maui; I read it at the library the island has in Lahaina, right on the waterfront, next to the Banyan Tree Park on Front Street. I thoroughly enjoyed it.

I ended up living in Maui by accident. While in New York City (where I stayed alternating between friends and my cousin Cher), the Australian embassy had put my working visa on hold, but I decided to continue my trip anyway; it didn't really matter where I was going. My friend Mary arranged my stay with Arthur, her hippie brother, at their brother-in-law's boat in Ala Wai Harbor* until I secured my own place.

My plan was to work in the islands, until I could continue toward Australia, where I was planning to settle down. I worked in Honolulu for a couple of months, installing cable television, until my position was given to the son of the owner: The devious manager who fired me gave me a lame excuse while avoiding my eyes.

At the moment, however, I was working part-time in another sailboat (the Solar Quest, a fifty foot long trimaran) with plans to get to know the area better, so losing my job didn't matter much. I was ready to sail, and sail we did!

o o o

We were a motley crew, we were. Wally was the elder, the captain, the owner of the boat, the man with the grizzled beard and scarce but long hair who was also a college professor. Tony was the second in command, a seasoned merchant marine resting between ships, who could fix just about anything. And Caroline, the English lady, an experienced sailor and maybe the best amongst us. She was sailing her way around the world to meet her boyfriend somewhere.

I also remember Cathy and Keith who were Wally's teenage offspring, and Arthur was also there with Lonnie, his Hawaiian girlfriend. And there was me, of course, the absolute beginner, still traveling with a suitcase, ties and suits—just in case.

I remember that during a strong gale one night, we lost Chicken, our cat. We lost many a thing during that summer. In fact, on a trip to Kauai we lost our rudder for a while, and the mizzen flopped to the deck on our return trip to Oahu. As if that was not enough, the main sail was torn at the boom and we had to reef it; consequently, we were able to enter Ala Wai Harbor only after our third attempt, due to our lacking in sails.

o o o

---

*Ala Wai Harbor marks the end of the Ala Wai Canal in Oahu, and the entrance to the Pacific Ocean.—Wikipedia

Being a beginner, my crew mates were letting me rest occasionally if I felt seasick; but one night, during a strong squall in which Wally called all hands on deck, I saw Caroline throwing up overboard as the Solar Quest pitched and tossed in dismay. She vomited while working, mind you, and so I learned the proper work ethics: Seasick or not, you did your share.

It was during that squall when I helped Caroline and Wally to install the jib's boom. I was learning.

Caroline was having trouble keeping the heavy boom steady for Wally. So after I locked it under my right arm, I maneuvered the boom around the mast, to a position that brought the sails to my help; it allowed me, with the wind's help, to press the opposite end of the boom against the mast, and to reduce its flailing about.

Doing that, I was able to hold it steady long enough for Wally to attach it to the mast. A flailing boom could have also knocked me overboard, to maybe disappear like our greatly missed white-cream tabby.

o o o

In spite of our stomach-turning difficulties, and the unhappy witch who was our next door neighbor at the pier, we enjoyed ourselves immensely that summer. We were constantly sailing from island to island, celebrating the clear blue skies, the windswept waves, and even the rain and squalls. We also caught tuna at times, and watched the dolphins play. And it was aboard the Solar Quest that I first saw the green flash.

It usually flashes at the end of a clear day, amid a calm ocean or a vast expanse of land, where nothing interrupts the view of the horizon. If you are alert you'll see an intense green flash at the precise moment the sun disappears beyond the horizon.

Tony told me that evening, that you can only see the green flash when you are surrounded by the ocean or the desert. But years later, I was dinning at one of the restaurants along the promenade in Puerto Vallarta, Mexico, and I saw an outstanding green flash. Since I still thought that you could only see it when amid the ocean, I thought that perhaps it had been an optical illusion. So I turned to my companions and asked nonchalantly:

"Have you ever seen the green flash?" They both said that they had just seen it that very moment.

o o o

But even summer has an end.

After helping my crew mates with minor boat repairs, and with the construction of two daggerboards to reduce sideways movement, I bid them goodbye early one morning in Maalaea Bay, in Maui, the island where I chose to stay. I remember the pungent smell of brine that morning, and a cool, soft breeze bringing the ocean mist to the surrounding trees; fluffy white clouds sprinkled the wide blue sky, and seagulls squabbled in the distance.

After bidding farewell to each of my crew mates (even Lonnie, who called me an asshole once, got a hug) I climbed on my laden bicycle and took my leave. I pedaled all the way to Hana and the seven pools, sweating my way over mountains galore, camping by the side of the road, to finally return to settle down in Lahaina. Alas, I missed the Haleakala volcano due to a lack of preparation and planning.

o o o

To survive in Lahaina, I set up camp on the outskirts, and tried a few cooking jobs in some of the plush hotels in Kaanapali, the famous tourist resort to which Lahaina is the gateway. I have to admit, however, that I was fired twice for being at odds with an always angry crew. It was disappointing because I wanted to learn the trade, but what an anger in that crew!

So I ended up driving the shuttle bus for Mr. P ____, the craziest, grumpiest, oldest boss I ever had, a workaholic, a ranter and a raver, a good soul trapped by greed and ego. He practically lived under his old, worn buses, fixing and tuning them. He would jeopardize the lives of his customers using buses in disrepair to make an extra buck.

But I didn't see much of him during my shift, and the job enabled me to secure a room close to Front Street and pay my bills. The room had a private entrance, and a shady yard with a few young mango trees, not a bad situation at all.

o o o

I made a few good friends in Lahaina. I remember Danny, a gypsy, an adventurer, a being with a zest for life, whom I met on the road to the seven pools. Before I secured my room, we camped together at the beach for a few days. I made many acquaintances through him (good and bad); he knew everybody.

Danny took off one day, heading to Mardi Gras in New Orleans; he loved the crowd, the music, the jostling of elbows, the wanton women. We never saw him again. Years later, I thought I saw him in San Francisco, at Fisherman's Wharf, a fleeting image amid the crowd, who didn't give me time to act before he was gone.

o o o

Perhaps it was *Tales of Power* by Castaneda—which encouraged me to practice inner silence—what helped me to find my hands in a dream for the first time. I found the book, which had been recently published, while browsing in the Front Street bookstore.

Whatever it was, something urged me to look at my hands while I was having a dream one night. As I looked at them they started to become gnarled and deformed, but I knew what to do. I looked for another object, and in front of me, I saw a low, black wrought-iron gate, which led onto a small grassless yard. I got immersed in detail while looking at the design and shape of the gate; I could see the smallest features and cracks with exceptional clarity.

I can't remember if I looked at my hands again, but I remember looking at a hedge; a hedge that bordered a low chain link fence, which surrounded a small white house. The house had a cozy little porch that stepped down onto the yard.

Suddenly, to the right of the house, a cat appeared. It looked fixedly into my eyes and quickly approached me—a strange behavior for a cat. It was an odd-looking grayish-yellow cat that never took his eyes from mine as he came near; then he jumped at me. Startled, I woke up.

Next day I was elated; I had not learned yet how to control elation or depression while facing life's challenges. I had not learned equanimity. Thus, that morning I was walking on air;

by my own volition, I had controlled a *dream*. I was beginning to reach my *dreaming attention*. Although I couldn't understand how, I had done it. I had broken undisclosed boundaries to discover new ways to perceive and act.

For the next few days, I tried unsuccessfully to do it again; I couldn't, but that didn't matter much. What mattered was that I had verified that it could be done; the *dreaming body* could act. So if in *dreaming* there is linear awareness, I pondered, where is this consciousness? Where is the mind?

o o o

Through my compatriot Rick, a jeweler who rented a small booth in a Front Street store, I met Jon, his brother-in-law. Jon had been a wanderer once, and was now returning to the states from Japan with his wife and toddler.

We were having dinner at Rick's house one night, and Jon charmed me with his stories about his travels through Mexico. Since I had recently been informed that Australia was definitively closing its doors to immigrants for the moment, I decided to visit Mexico.

o o o

I left my bicycle with Rick and Dina, and boarded a plane to the mainland. I don't remember exactly where I landed, but I ended up in Tucson, Arizona, where I stayed with friends of Jon for a couple of days. Then, I was on my own again. I also remember catching the flu and calling my friend Jane from a downtown hotel; we had also met in Maui.

After a twenty-four hour bus ride, under siege by a cold draft, I arrived at Jane's house in Palo Alto, California seriously sick. She nursed me back to health though, and we traveled through California and Arizona, visiting Yosemite and the Grand Canyon before entering Mexico through the Nogales border. We parted company in Hermosillo, Sonora. Thus, I became a vagabond in Mexico.

o o o

My experiences in Mexico as a working vagabond were related in my book *A Vagabond in Mexico,* so I will not delve into them here. I will tell you, however, that in Mexico I experienced life from many different perspectives. At the beginning, the experience was light and enjoyable. At the end, having to make a living working as an illegal immigrant in a third world country proved extremely hard. It altered my awareness.

It was while living in Mexico, when I did *dreaming* for a second time. It happened while I was working in Guaymas, living in a shabby, moldering laundry room behind the house of my employer.

I found my hands in a dream, and when I looked up, I found myself in a large house with several rooms along a deep corridor. I was standing amid a small living room; an old sofa with gray cushions and a few matching chairs were the only pieces of furniture.

I knew that I was *dreaming,* so I drifted down the corridor to see what I could find. It seemed that I was in a Mexican house. I was trying to hold the *dream* for as long as possible, while looking at everything, for practice in *dreaming* is the key to develop your *dreaming body.*

Suddenly a mouse came out of nowhere. Its behavior, like the cat's behavior in my first *dreaming* experience, was obviously meant to catch my attention. After moving slowly toward me, it ran and started to jump up and down. Then it jumped upon me. Again, I woke up startled.

At the time, I couldn't fathom what these animals were; I was not aware yet of the inorganic beings (allies) who roam the *dreaming* realm. I decided to ignore the apparitions in the future by looking at my hands instead.

o o o

When my time in Mexico ended, I crossed the border in Nogales, to settle in Tucson while I sorted things out. Tucson stands amid the Sonoran Desert, surrounded by giant saguaros and flanked by magnificent peaks; it is the land of the Palo Verde trees; the land where Castaneda met don Juan.

And it was in Tucson, while working as a truck driver delivering doors to construction sites, where I was able to corroborate fully my *dreaming* location. That night, after finding my hands in a dream, I found myself in the kitchen of the cottage that I rented close to the University of Arizona at 1030 E. Lee Street. I inspected the sink in front of me carefully. It was my sink exactly! I was in my kitchen. Other than everything being a little bigger than usual (like Castaneda describes himself) it was my place.

I was dumbfounded, so I screwed up; the room where I slept was next to the kitchen, but it didn't cross my mind to look inside to see myself asleep. Instead, I "walked" toward my living room, moving carefully in the dimness, as if I could bump into something. I passed my refrigerator, entered the living room, and "walked" past the heater embedded in the wall. I also "walked" around the low, long wooden table in the center of the room.

In those days, I related to my *dreaming body* as if it was my physical body, so I "walked" or tried to open doors, as if my *dreaming body* had matter. The next thing I did was to sit down on the sofa while looking at everything in awe.

Everything was there, just as I had left it when I went to sleep. Next day, I concluded that I had been sitting on my sofa, in my living room, while I had been sleeping on my bed, in my room.

And I was excited but also chagrined; I had missed the opportunity to look at myself sleeping. One of the main goals of *dreaming* is to establish that you definitely are in two places at once. Then, with much practice, the *dreaming body* can *intend* a physical body who can act in our daily world. The two locations can be equally real, and either of them can be maintained and the other discarded; something that might come in handy if you are ever in a tight spot.

But anyway (and there was no doubt in my mind) I had been *there,* roaming my cottage, *while I slept in my room!* Years later in Los Angeles CA, while exchanging thoughts with a fellow *dreamer,* at the only Cleargreen[†] workshop I ever attended, she told me that once she had met with her neighbor in her backyard

---

[†] Cleargreen Inc. was founded by Castaneda to clarify his teachings through workshops, and for the practice of "tensegrity," magical passes. (Chapter 7)

while both had been *dreaming*. The Brihadaranyaka Upanishad[‡] (The Forest of Wisdom) says that in the *dreaming* state, when one is sleeping, the shining Self keeps the body alive with the vital force of prana and wanders wherever he wills.

o o o

But in spite of my *dreaming,* I have to admit, for the challenge of acquiring wisdom is quite a part of this journey, that in those days I was quite an asshole. My self-importance was still high and I was easily offended. I didn't know how to control my temper with the petty tyrants of the world, so in anger one day, I quit my job as truck driver after a disagreement with my boss.

My next job as a cook's helper didn't last long either. At the end of my first week, on Friday night, the owner politely told me not to come back because "I wasn't blending with the crew." It was true. In my opinion, just like in Kaanapali, the crew was angrily insane. Thus, I was able to collect unemployment, and I started to do leather work to make some extra money.

But to keep on the subject of being a jackass, I have to add that with my girlfriends I wasn't much better, always trying to impose my will, always unable to consider them friends and growing human beings. I remember Barbara in particular, who without saying a word, made me feel like shit when she dumped me. I will not explain further; it was thoroughly embarrassing. Suffice it to say that she was right.

Egomania, however, is a condition that at the very least causes tunnel vision and at the very worst total blindness, I was not aware of my ego being a problem—everybody else was wrong, I was right. So I decided to leave. I'd go to South America and visit my sister in Ecuador, where I could perhaps settle down if I liked it. In other words, at the time, I was changing physical circumstances while, despite Don Juan's teachings, working minimally on my inner development; I couldn't smell the shit in my own pockets.

[‡]The Upanishads contain the Vedas, the most ancient Hindu scriptures, containing truths believed to have been revealed directly to seers among the early Aryans in India.

It is also true that, to a certain extent, my restlessness was probably also due to the fact that my *dreaming body* was awakening. I was doing things that I couldn't communicate readily or understand fully, and I was keeping it all to myself, for I didn't know how to relate to it, or if I should talk about it at all. I was no longer relating to the world as an average man, but I didn't know how to act in my new world, with my new perspective. I was beginning to think that I was special; I needed guidance.

o   o   o

The Sonoran Desert has an allure of its own, perhaps because of its giant saguaros and unique Palo Verde trees, which gleam yellow during spring. It is a magical place of overpowering size and extreme heat.

I often hiked from Tucson to my favorite *places of power,* nurturing places. One day, as I hiked toward Sabino Canyon, I stopped to rest. I propped up two rocks about 4 inches long close to each other. I crossed my eyes as I focused on their shadows.

Where the shadows merge another world was form, a world with its own depth and shapes. I was using don Juan's technique to enlarge the world by reducing it. At the time, I didn't know that I could have entered that world.

o   o   o

In Tucson I started to write *A Vagabond in Mexico.* I had been an avid reader and writer since I was an adolescent, and after I finished a two year stint in the army, I studied creative writing and was able to publish a couple of articles.

So when I left, I took the first draft of the manuscript with me, to finish it wherever I could. As on my first trip to Mexico, my possessions were few, so I packed everything into my now orange backpack and headed south.

o   o   o

My folks in Guaymas (the family who gave me shelter when I was a working vagabond in Mexico) were building a sturdy brand new home in masonry. I had brought them a few things that would fit in their new pad.

Doña Rebecca had been seriously sick the year before, but she had recovered and was well now. Carlitos was turning into a responsible young man. Goliad was getting old but he remembered me; he did not chase cats anymore. Doña Rebecca rocked the new house-in-progress with hilarious memories—like the time diarrhea attacked me in the middle of the night, and I was not able to reach the outhouse.

After leaving Guaymas, I traversed the country by bus to Mexico City from where I took a plane to Quito, Ecuador. Eventually, I lost touch. I have not seen them since.

I never saw Maria Elena again.

Chapter 2

Hostile Allies

The passageway into the world of shamans opens up after the warrior has learned to shut off his internal dialogue.—don Juan

Quito, the capital of Ecuador, is perched 9500 feet above sea level upon the Andes Mountains. When I arrived, a small plane had recently missed the runway, due to bad weather, and crashed into the surrounding slopes of the Pichincha.* So a few days after my arrival, my sister Carla and her friends organized a hike up to the crash site, to see the charred remains of the plane. As a result, I had the opportunity to enjoy a spectacular view of Quito, surrounded by the magnificent peaks of the Andes.

o o o

Sorcerers do not particularly impress Daniel, my brother in law. The possibility that *brujos* may have a different system of cognition to which they may arrive by a sophisticated and complex system of behavior is of no concern at all to him or my sister. Nevertheless, while in Ecuador, I remember having a conversation with him in which he told me about an experience his father had with the double, the *other*. His father, he said, *se desdoblo*.

---

[1]The Guagua Pichincha volcano is located 14 kilometers from Quito; it erupted as recently as 1999.—Wikipedia

It happened a day that his father had been working at the family's ranch all day long. When he returned he was so tired that he led his horse to the stable but neglected to feed him. Exhausted, don Manuel went to bed and fell asleep. Remorse, however, wouldn't allow him the needed rest; around midnight he awoke from restless sleep. He decided to get up, go to the stable, and feed the horse.

As he approached the building though, he saw that the lights were on, which was strange, and heard noises. He was on edge, and upon opening the door he almost jumped out of his boots. There, in the stable, feeding his horse, he saw himself. For a moment he stood aghast.

But he knew better than to interfere. He closed the door and went back to bed. Now he would be able to sleep; the horse had been fed, as he was able to corroborate the next morning. My brother in law explained that that night his father *se desdobló*; he was in two places at once.

My brother-in-law also told me about a town in Ecuador called *el pueblo de los brujos,* the town of the sorcerers. It was named so because of the great amount of sorcerers that lived there. Maybe I should have visited the town, but I didn't; I had understood from what I had read and heard that their arts were barred to strangers and solicitors. Besides, I had learned during my travels in Mexico, that some *brujos* are just petty manipulators. The road, I figured, would take me to wherever I had to go; when the student is ready the teacher appears.

o o o

It was in South America, however, where I really crossed the point of no return. Settling in Ecuador was an attractive possibility, but fate intervened. Some correspondence I had with my folks, opened my eyes to the fact that even from a distance they were trying to run my race, to direct my life; and subtly, I was still clinging to my past, to who I had been. So I decided to take my leave.

The visit had been fun. I had been impressed by the beauty of Ecuador, but I really couldn't stay, and the road was beckoning with secrets to reveal. After saying (and writing) good-bye to everyone, I accepted 200 dollars from my sister, and let the road swallow me. I literally disappeared. For the next 15 years nobody heard from me; nobody knew my whereabouts. The omens along the road would decide my fate.[†]

Not knowing exactly what to do, for I didn't have enough money to get anywhere in particular, I followed the road north. At the border with Colombia, I met with my first serious obstacle: not having enough money to qualify for a tourist visa.

I was in luck though, a taxi driver came to my rescue. Apparently he had noticed my comings and goings, and perhaps my demeanor, my bedraggled outfit, and my tattered straw hat suggested that I was in need of assistance. He approached me.

"Yo le hago la gauchada," he said, after I explained my predicament.

And he did; for 15 dollars he produced a tourist visa good for three months—no questions asked. What can I tell you? The man had connections; he took me to a house on the outskirts, and while I waited in the car he procured all the necessary documents. I thanked him from the bottom of my heart, and decided to cross Colombia as fast as I could; for it was a country at war, not a safe place to work or engage in any lucrative enterprise without proper documentation.

o o o

Throughout my mountainous bus trip, I remember mainly jungles with thick, lush vegetation. I also remember a boulevard in Bogota, the Capital, where a wide variety of flowers were being sold in stands, along a wide walkway that divided the thoroughfare's four lanes. Perhaps it was the month of May.

I can also recall the friendly welcome I received, from the ladies I met, using the subterfuge of asking for directions. So attractive and inviting were they that I was seriously tempted to stay, but Colombia is a country in perennial conflict.

Not for nothing everyone I met in Bogota—where I stayed a few days with friends of my sister—advised me to carry my papers with me always; in a war zone, everyone is a suspect.

[†]According to ancient Indian custom, when a man renounces his past he becomes a new person altogether, *never to go home again.*

In fact, the troops stopped and rudely searched me a couple of times. I didn't blame them though, for a well known politician had been recently murdered in his own home, and I probably looked like a guerrilla fighter.

It was also good advice to keep my belongings continuously in sight. In Colombia I lost an amulet that I kept in a small leather pouch in a pocket of my backpack. It just disappeared. In this respect Colombia is just like the YMCA in Mission Valley, CA, where you can even lose your slippers in the locker room if you lose sight of them for a millisecond.

In Colombia, however, the thieves had a routine. I saw them in action myself, in broad daylight, while traveling by train to the port of Santa Marta.‡ I heard a stewardess, explaining to another passenger what I had just witnessed.

The thieves climb aboard the train during routine stops, and, if you are the intended victim, the young hoods drift casually toward you, and swiftly getting a hold of your watch, or your necklace, they yank it off your person, and flee to safety by jumping off the train and disappearing into the bustling crowd. I also saw this happen one night amid a busy street in Acapulco, Mexico; the thieves vanished.

o o o

I made a detour. I flew to the island of San Andres to avoid Nicaragua, where an army of rebels was fighting to oust the dictator Somoza.

o o o

The reason I found San Andres unique was not its scuba diving locations, or my nightly battle against the swarming droves of whizzing, relentless mosquitoes while camping at the beach. What I saw in San Andres, which I had never seen anywhere else, was the complete lack of racial discrimination in the people's interactions.

There is usually a certain reserve between races even when there is acceptance and friendship. Even when a person of a

---

‡ The first Spanish City founded in South America.

different race is being friendly in casual contact, I can always hear between the lines:

"You're not my kind, be aware."

In San Andres, regardless of who I was speaking to, I couldn't detect that at all; it just wasn't there. It is true that I was only there for a couple of weeks, and therefore, I might be wrong in my assessment; but let me tell you that there was also a remarkable kindness in them.

I was sitting down on the sidewalk once, on the curb, by the stairwell of a humble home, and a woman climbed down the stairs with a plate of food for me. I had never seen her before and I never saw her again. I guess she figured (due probably to my appearance) that I didn't have a good situation.

And she was right, by the time I got to Guatemala I was nearly broke again; somehow, it was time to make some dough. Through the traveler's grapevine, I learned that travelers, from all over the world, met and exchanged news in Panajachel, a well-known tourist town located along the shores of the famous Lake Atitlan.

o o o

A Guatemalan couple, the hippie young owners of a quaint leather shop downtown, were kind enough to hire me; they even let me sleep in their living room for a couple of days. Thus, I thought my luck was changing for the better in Panajachel, but on payday the couple refused to pay me for my work, or for the items I had made for them with leather that I had brought from Ecuador.

I was disgusted by their lack of integrity, so I left disgruntled. At the time, I was still a vengeful egomaniac, so I held a grudge for quite a while, refusing to shake the man's hand a couple of times when we met by chance. Years later, I saw him in Mexico, on the lam, escaping from a country torn by war; and I wondered if perhaps, due to that traumatic experience, his outlook on life might have been altered a bit.

o o o

The man I worked for next was in need of a harrowing experience himself. Jose had a small lumberyard, and he was planning to pay me two quetzals a day, a miserable sum with which I wouldn't have been able to subsist. Therefore, thinking I was being ingenious, I decided to ask him if I could work for room and board.

Jose agreed to let me sleep in the lumber shed. And for two days the family had their morbid fun watching me eat their serving: a watery soup with no aroma, flavor or substance. It did have a meatless bone and a few beans, and was accompanied by a couple of scrawny, old tortillas.

They didn't eat with me; they had already eaten. They just watched me eat with a sardonic look on their face. I never understood their malice.

My coworkers, two young Mayans who were smart enough to bring their own lunch, weren't faring much better. They were treated like beasts of burden at times, and given ponderous loads of lumber to be carried over great distances.

These men, mind you, were small in stature but extremely strong, and were accustomed to hard work. They carried these hefty loads of lumber by tying the bundles at opposite ends with a strap. They then secured the strap around their foreheads, and lifted the load to their lower back, while bending the body slightly forward. In this manner, distributing the weight evenly, and supporting it with their heads and neck, they were able to walk great distances to deliver their cargo.

I tried to help them once, but, when I realized that we were hiking quite far into the jungle with the heavy load, I dropped the lumber I was carrying on my shoulder, went back to the shop, and asked Jose if we could use his pickup truck. He ordered me not to help them; he didn't want to spoil the "Indians."

Such is the world of the ego, isn't it? His own Indian ancestry was obvious.

○ ○ ○

Quitting that job was a survival tactic.

I managed to make a similar deal at a small hostel on the outskirts of town. The place was managed by Twinkle, an American hippie.

After a few days, however, she explained that I was eating more than she could afford to pay me. I had to go. And I have to admit that, being behind in my meals, I *was* eating a lot. Besides, on one occasion, I made her cringe in her chair when, much to her chagrin, I told her that she was smoking dope in excess.

I had to go!

Next morning, while I drifted down the main road toward the lake after a frugal breakfast, I pondered what to do. I was seriously thinking that the count remaining on my days was not high at all, when suddenly a memory burst forth to my rescue.

During my stay in the island of San Andres, while camping at the beach, I met a Colombian hippie[§] who let me crash in his place for a couple of days. In exchange, I helped him to sell his crafts on the beach. While working with him, he taught me how to make a puzzle by twisting and hooking a couple of nails. I decided then that that was that. That was what I had to do to earn some dough.

Thus, I went to the welding shop in Panajachel, and asked the owner to forge the tool that I needed to make the puzzles. This young man was Jose's brother, but unlike Jose he was a decent man, and realizing that I was barely staying alive, he refused to collect his dues. I gave him the necessary instructions.

And so, I became a peddler; I started selling puzzles at the beach in Lake Atitlan. I also found Jucanya, the village located across the river[**] (I never saw water in that river). At the village, I started renting a thatched hut for fifty cents a day.

o o o

The farming village of Jucanya is just a few minutes walk from Panajachel; it is the Mayan part of town, a suburb con-

---

[§]That man owned a copy of *Journey to Ixtlan* by Carlos Castaneda; his bible, he said.

[**]In Cakchiquel, the local language, the word *jucanya* means "the other side of the river."

sisting of small adobe huts with thatched roofs. The residents use a network of irrigation ditches to water their crops, mainly corn. They rent huts to supplement their income.

My one-room adobe hut had a small wooden table, a folding wooden chair, a firewood stove and a floor of dirt. A few wooden boards propped by adobe bricks, became the bed where I placed my sleeping bag. I remember that the hut had two windows and a door, but neither the door nor the windows allowed much light in.

During the morning, however, sun rays slanted in through the window that faced the trail. I usually had breakfast by that window, and after I washed my dishes, I sat again at the table to do my day's work, while watching my neighbors' comings and goings, and chatting with them at times.

o o o

My neighbor explained that I was to look for a certain herb, which was common in the area, and he showed me a few leaves that he had collected himself. To make sure I had the right plant, I had to grind its leaves on the palms of my hands and catch a whiff of its smell, the smell of skunk.

My sore throat spurred me on to find the herbs. That night I boiled the roots and leaves for a few minutes, as directed; and before going to bed, I drank most of the preparation. Then I soaked a bandana in the remains, wrung it, and wrapped it around my throat. The next morning, I was well.

o o o

Lake Atitlan is nestled among the volcanoes of Central America, and it is world famous for its natural beauty; it is said to be the most beautiful lake in the world. But I had to bathe and do my laundry somewhere, and all the natives did their laundry in Lake Atitlan, so I followed suit. I remember that the women would laugh at me, for Mayan men don't do laundry.

But, who cared? After I started selling my puzzles at the beach, I was able to say that I was (barely) making a living. I had, to some degree, a better situation.

In truth, I was still wondering if I would survive, for when the wind rose, the tourists disappeared as if swallowed by the lake, and sales dropped to zero. When the wind was up in arms, I would always see, when I crossed the huge log that spanned the dry riverbed, a low long cloud nestled along the inland horizon. Whenever I saw that cloud cradled among the mountains, I knew that if the wind was not blowing yet, it would soon be. Wind or no wind, I would go to work, for I needed whatever monies I could make.

o o o

If you would have crossed the wide, dry river bed when coming from Jucanya, and followed the asphalt road to meet the main road in town, you would have passed the welding shop to your left. Upon turning right onto the main road, you would have found the market. Farther up, half a block down a connecting dirt road, stood the health food store and restaurant. The jungle loomed in the distance, encasing the town like a magical cocoon.

Upon turning left and walking downhill, however, you would have reached downtown, where the shops, hotels, restaurants and the bakery [tt] were located. Veering then to your left and following the road toward the beach, you would have passed some private houses, a trailer park, and many shops selling Guatemalan crafts. I remember that every now and then, I would stop at one of the shops to chat with Emilito, the owner.

o o o

There lived in Panajachel a wandering young orphan who was now struggling on her own to raise her nine-year-old child, a son conceived out of wedlock. It was said in town that she was also recovering from a recently failed liaison; a liaison that apparently failed due to her possessiveness.

One day that I was at the lake, I saw her sunning herself on the beach while I struggled to sell; and early that evening, as I was leaving the bakery, she asked me for a piece of bread, forcing me to confront a moral dilemma: That loaf of bread

---

[tt]That bakery sold the best banana bread I have ever had, for 50 cents a loaf; it saved my life.

was my supper and my breakfast. I said *no*. Should I have given her a piece of bread?

But I think she understood; she never held a grudge. A day or so later our paths crossed as she and her son were coming from the lake. We stood in mottled sunshine that morning, under a sky partly covered with fluffy, grayish-white clouds. I gave her kid a puzzle.

The kid was obviously thrilled and immediately plunged into the challenge of trying to separate the nails. She thanked me, and they continued on their way to town. That was the last time I saw them; she waved good-bye as they diminished in the distance, the child still immersed in his challenge. I can see them now.

A couple of years later, while in Mexico, I heard from Dario, a fellow traveler whom I had also met in Panajachel while he was managing the trailer park, that she had been found dead on the road. I was stunned, and saddened. Remorse smote me.

I thought about the bread; the bread I didn't give her. Shouldn't we give without considering the merits of the recipient? I would have survived anyway. Besides, what chains had she been dragging from her orphaned childhood that nobody knew about? How emotionally stressed had she been due to her failed relationship? She was a lost soul at the moment; she needed friends. I had played judge.

I forgave myself, however, and I forgave her. I hope her child survived the ruthless war that, unbeknownst to us, was coming.

o o o

After about two weeks in Panajachel I had the good fortune to meet a compatriot, a young, outgoing hippie who was also a craftsman. Upon learning my situation he taught me how to weave string-art jewelry; it was indeed art, and so inexpensive to do that it was easy to sell for a good profit. All I needed was copper wire, thread, and a few simple tools that I could buy in the town of Solola, a few miles away. That was a turning point.

During my first day selling jewelry I made 13 dollars, which in Guatemala was good money for a day's work. Peddling that jewelry for the next two weeks, I was able to make enough money to go to Guatemala City and extend my tourist visa for three more months. I even bought a new handcrafted leather hat, a fedora.

Three months later, I had enough money to cross the border into Mexico. I hitchhiked from the border, and the two college students who gave me a lift, directed me to what they called, "a hot spot." They explained that due to the high volume of tourists, it was an excellent place to sell my work; the city was called Cuernavaca.

The students drop me off in front of the main square in the city of Tuxtla Gutierrez, where I was able to sell enough jewelry to take care of my expenses. The omens were good.

o o o

The encounter happened unexpectedly.

As fortune had it, I had to take the last and worst room in a small hotel somewhere; I can't remember the name of the town. I do remember the room, however, as one of the worst I have ever stayed in: a dark and gloomy cubby without windows, crammed with furniture that impaired every one of my movements. The stagnant air reeked of dust and mildew. The bed had a deep depression in the middle, and to protect my back, I had to sleep on the outer edge.

I figure that my odd, cramped surroundings helped me stop my internal dialogue that night, and I had my first meeting with the inorganic beings who are hostile to us; the ones that, just like Castaneda explained years *later,* disguise themselves as relatives and friends.

In that *dreaming,* I found myself in a dark, ghostly house that was empty of furniture and lacked windows. I peered into an open room and saw my sister lying on a high, black antique bed made of wrought iron. Her face and arms had a ghastly pallor; she seemed dead.

Suddenly, she rose on her elbows, and gaping at me with a blank look, she beckoned me to come near. It was a frightening and threatening sight; it was my sister, but it wasn't. I felt the apparition meant harm. I started retreating, preparing to flee, but I didn't have to, for my *dreaming attention* left me. I found myself back in that dismal room, at the edge of that lumpy bed. Baffled, I fell asleep again.

Next day, I thought that maybe my sister was ill, or perhaps dead. I thought to call her but I decided to wait for a second dream; I had read or heard somewhere that if dreams mean to tell you something they repeat themselves. Besides, at the moment, I wanted to cut all links with my family, so I didn't want to reveal my whereabouts. But I felt uneasy; I couldn't figure out what, or who, I was meeting when *dreaming*. I couldn't understand.

The *dream* didn't repeat itself, but weeks later, in Cuernavaca, I had a similar experience. I found myself at the door of a huge, eerily somber room in which furniture and windows were missing again; the entity involved was not visible at first, but I could feel its presence.

Suddenly, she appeared to my right; it was a middle-age woman sitting down on a rocking chair. Her features were my mother's but not quite; her hair was combed towards the back in a way that my mother wouldn't have combed it. Her countenance was a cruel, ignoble mask.

Either I was moving left or the rocking chair was swiveling to the right. Again, I knew that whoever was sitting down on that rocking chair meant harm. I cautiously started retreating and she vanished.

Chapter 3

The Enemy Within

You are the screen, the Self has created the ego, the ego has its accretions of thoughts, which are displayed as the world. . . . In reality, all these are nothing but the Self. Nothing but the Self exists.—Be As You Are: The teachings of Sri Ramana Maharshi

The afternoon sun was beginning to cast the giant shadow of evening upon the dusty downtown streets of Cuernavaca. I walked downhill toward the center of town, leaving behind the crowded bus station filled with bawling infants and angry blaring horns. I walked in earnest, with anticipation, welcoming the new sights and smells; the mouth watering smells emanating from the *carne asada* and onions, frying in mobile food stands edging the sidewalks.

Without delay, I took up residence in an inexpensive downtown hotel. I remember it was about four o'clock. I remember because the moment I entered my room, I dropped my backpack, grabbed my recently made jewelry, and rushed out to find a place and set up shop before dusk.

In a period of about two hours, standing on a street corner close to the main plaza, I sold every piece I had. Thus, I had a good dinner that night, the first of many to come.

o o o

Not for nothing is Cuernavaca known as the city of eternal spring; the aromas of the season and the song of birds and mariachis are constantly in the air; the bougainvilleas are always blooming, and the average temperature throughout the year is 80° Fahrenheit. Surrounded by rolling hills and cut by narrow, cobbled streets, Cuernavaca is a charming colonial remnant just an hour away from the traffic and pollution of Mexico City.

During my year stay, the plaza and the surrounding restaurants were always teeming with visitors, especially during weekends. Therefore, business was good in Cuernavaca, and I was able to relax. And after I got rid of some parasites, which I had been unknowingly hosting for some time, I recovered the weight I had lost on the road.

Cuernavaca's vibrant life and warm climate attracts visitors from all over the world. Sometimes these foreigners are from as far away as Texas.

o o o

Michelle had just finished dinner early one night in one of the spacious restaurants I visited while selling my string-art jewelry. She was relaxing at her table with her folks, and she bought one of my pendants.

Thus, we met! And for a while we were planning to travel by land all the way to Brazil.

Although she could have been on the cover of *Seventeen*, Michelle had a mature demeanor and a down-to-earth attitude with a sense of humor to match. I still remember her utterly hilarious comments made with deadpan countenance, and her mother's bewildered questions from the kitchen as we burst out laughing in the living room about something or other.

We didn't quite travel to Brazil. But we had ice cream occasionally. We went swimming and dinning. We strolled hand in hand to the square downtown, and watched Mexican movies so that she could learn Spanish. We made an odd couple, I am sure we did; except for my hat and boots, my extensive wardrobe could always fit in my backpack: jeans and matching Guatemalan hand woven shirts. But it didn't matter; we loved each other—for a while.

And if it is true that she dumped me after her visit to grandma in Texas (I knew that that visit would test her resolve), it is also true that she was too young to make a serious commitment yet. Besides, vagabonds are not favorites of their mothers-in-law (or grandmas-in-law for that matter) even if they have a good sense of humor, for they can take their daughters to distant lands, perhaps forever.

o   o   o

After about five months of living in Cuernavaca, I returned briefly to Guatemala. In those days, a tourist visa expired in six months, and you had to leave the country for at least a few days. During that visit to Guatemala, around the year of 1979, I noticed that the soldiers at the military checkpoints were under stress, and soon after I returned to Cuernavaca a bloody revolution* erupted in the country, making that my last visit to that Central American country.

During my stay in Panajachel, I used to listen to a duo of guitar players from Canada, two brothers who sometimes played in the health food store's restaurant at night. One of my favorite songs in their repertoire was *The Boxer*. And when making my last exit, a few of the song's lyrics came to mind:

"Lord I'm leaving, I am leaving, but the fighter still remains . . ."

I never returned to Guatemala.

o   o   o

Nevertheless, for years I led quite a nomadic life, traveling between Mexico, Central America (Belize) and the U.S. while selling my crafts. My new lifestyle was so different from what I had been used to, that I was definitely developing a new way of perceiving. My routines were disrupted frequently, and my life was practically always on the line; so I had to take responsibility for every act, and the impermanence of things and situations was obvious. Traveling fosters non-attachment, and travelers are a living symbol of impermanence.

---

* It left more than 200,000 civilians dead or "disappeared," and the poorly armed rebels were eventually defeated.

o o o

It was risky to sell my crafts in port cities or towns because of *La Migra;* immigration was ubiquitous there. I met with them while selling on the beach in San Blas, in the State of Nayarit. Luckily, it was Sunday, and the officer wasn't working that day. He was having lunch with his wife.

When I told him I was from Sonora but my papers were in my hotel, he didn't quite believe me, but he cut me some slack. He said that it was his day off, but that I'd better be out of town by Monday if I couldn't show valid papers. Otherwise, things wouldn't go well for me. His wife looked at me sympathetically and nodded; there was a warning in her nod. I thanked them.

I left town.

o o o

Learning to fly with the *dreaming body* happened spontaneously. It happened while working in the pleasant hamlet of Barra de Navidad, close to Puerto Vallarta. Somehow, while *dreaming,* something urged me to try, although it had never crossed my mind that it could be done.

In that *dreaming* I found myself in a little plaza in Melaque, the neighboring town. I was still in the habit of thinking that I had a physical body when I was *dreaming.* So I grabbed the flagpole, or a pole of some sort, and tried to pull myself up and away from the ground; I couldn't of course. Suddenly, I realized that *I* didn't have any substance, pulling myself up was absurd.

The moment the realization struck me, I let go. I *intended* myself up and up I went. I found myself in the air, higher and higher. I thought speed, and there it was: speed, and what a speed! I was rocketing through the dark night. It was exhilarating!

Suddenly, I was fearful, wondering if I would be able to stop, and the fear made me come to a complete halt. I looked down and saw the lights of a small town in the distant mountains below. I was not on the coast anymore.

I *intended* my descent, and I think I landed in Taxco. I couldn't verify my supposition, for my *dreaming* energy was waning. But the place where I landed looked familiar; it looked like the terrace of a hotel where I used to stay when I went there on business.

The experience was exhilarating, and it taught me that we can fly, just like we can go through a wall, in our *dreaming bodies*. A few days later I repeated the experience, but I stayed close to the ground. I saw a man riding a bicycle below me. It seemed to be the main street in Barra de Navidad, but it was dark, so I couldn't be sure.

o   o   o

It also happened while living in Barra, that I came across another kind of ally. In this *dreaming* episode, I found myself out in the countryside, somewhere in the area it seemed. In the dark of night, I tried to orient myself. I saw a small house under construction in an open field. I approached and entered it. In the darkness, I could barely distinguish a floor of dirt strewn with debris and mounds of sand. In the darkness, a surprise awaited.

I looked up to descry two long shapes hovering about a foot above the ground. They were to my right some ten feet away. I was startled, but they didn't seem hostile. I saw them as long, dull energy fields a little taller than I was. It was obvious that they were aware of me, as I was aware of them. I couldn't figure out who, or what, they were.

We *looked* at each other for a few moments. They seemed to be appraising me without malice, just as I was appraising them. I did not know what to do, or how to communicate, or even if I should communicate. I was cautiously retreating when they vanished.

o   o   o

Mysteriously, during my stay in Barra de Navidad, my *dreaming* activity increased.

I had understood that being close to large bodies of water was an obstacle to *dreaming,* but in my case that didn't seem to apply. Barra de Navidad is located between the Pacific Ocean and a large lagoon: *Laguna de Navidad.* Nevertheless, I could randomly do *dreaming* almost three or four times a week without any effort on my part.

But I was uncertain. I didn't know what to do about the beings I was meeting. I decided to use the fifth principle of the *art of stalking*: In the face of insurmountable odds retreat and appraise your situation.

As a consequence, my *dreaming* came almost to a halt; it became sporadic. I did not see any more inorganic beings for a long time. But I think I made the right decision; for later, when *The Art of Dreaming* was published, I learned that although inorganic beings can be of great help as guides if you follow them to their world, they can also trap us there, for they crave our energy.

o o o

A dark cloud settled over Barra de Navidad for some time; a friend died. His family owned one of the restaurants along the beach, where I used to sell my crafts. I gave his wife my sincere condolences.

They had been a middle-aged couple with grown children, who used to stroll downtown, holding hands like newlyweds. He died in his sleep, right beside her, apparently from heart failure.

At length, the cloud drifted away.

o o o

At times it is difficult to write when you are on the road, especially when the future is uncertain, but I finally finished and polished the main draft for *A Vagabond in Mexico* in San Miguel de Allende, in the mountains of the state of Guanajuato, during the summer of 1984. I remember that I used to write in the cozy little library located in *la calle Insurgentes*.

I usually worked in the sunny center patio, or in the main room: The room with the huge, unabridged English dictionary and the grand wooden table. I heard that now *la biblioteca* has computers, a restaurant and other amenities, and it is the second largest bilingual library in Mexico.

American expatriates founded *la biblioteca,* I heard.

o o o

San Miguel de Allende, a Mecca for the Arts, nestles on a hill and extends down onto a valley. It has a sizable foreign community, which lends a cosmopolitan flavor to the town, but it has also been declared a national monument, so it is still clearly a Mexican city. I remember that business was excellent on weekends, at *el jardin* (the plaza). I also remember that the town had the longest and wildest celebrations I have ever seen, with incredible fireworks.

It was during one of these celebrations that I witnessed something remarkable. It happened a Sunday afternoon, as I walked at leisure while selling my crafts. The town swarmed with people. The streets were littered with cans and reeking of beer. The crowd at the plaza had been drinking and it was beginning to show.

Suddenly, I descried something in the air, rocketing from the opposite side, arcing across the sky. It was a beer can! And it had to be full to be able to travel that high and that fast. I stared helplessly at the descending projectile; a warning shout would have been useless.

A riot was just about to start; it was inevitable. And I knew that the local police force would be inadequate to handle the situation; the town would be wrecked and many people hurt before help could be summoned.

The beer can hit somebody about forty feet away to my right, and as if lightning had struck in their midst, the crowd flared! But showing remarkable restrain, the man hit by the can did not retaliate. Instead, he started shouting and gesticulating toward both sides, exhorting everyone to calm down.

Miraculously, it worked! I don't know how. I don't know who he was either; he appeared to be just an ordinary citizen. But that man did not react; he acted. Mastering himself, he prevented a riot in the cobblestone streets of the historic colonial town of San Miguel de Allende, Guanajuato. I was a witness.

∘ ∘ ∘

After finishing my manuscript, I found myself at a crossroads. I had to decide whether to travel north, back to the states, to try to publish it, or wait and go south all the way to Brazil. I had the wanderlust. I had taken a liking to my independent nomadic life, and I had the urge to get to know South

America better, to go all the way to Rio de Janeiro. Even without Michelle it would have been an interesting journey.

o o o

When facing an uncertain fate, or a misfortune, I relax, appraise the situation, and plan a course of action. So late that autumn, although winters are moderate in San Miguel, I traveled to Zipolite, a small village on the coast of the state of Oaxaca, to try to solve my dilemma. It took me about a month to make a decision, but I was not in a hurry; in tropical Mexico, winter is the best time to enjoy the Pacific Ocean.

I chose the place due to its seclusion. I had been to Zipolite before, when its only connection to Puerto Angel and civilization had been a bumpy, rutted dirt road, a tortuous obstacle course. It was a rustic, unassuming village sans hotels or motels, where the residents rented hammocks to the travelers in their ramadas. It was a haven frequented mostly by hippies and wandering travelers like myself in search of something or other.

In those days, the village was composed of a few shacks lined along a beach, which extended until it reached a high cliff where Gloria's place was located. Electricity was nonexistent, so at night only the drums around the campfires would compete with the roaring phosphorescent surf; at night you could see Ursa Minor in the sky, pointing at the North Star, and shooting stars were a common sight.

Be advised though, the beach has treacherous rocks, deadly rip tides and no lifeguards; you swim at your own risk. Early one morning, I bumped into a drowned young man, at peace, purple, right on the beach where the tide had laid him down, surrounded by some of the soldiers who were stationed in town—apparently a European traveler who unwisely disregarded the ocean's warnings. Indeed, body surfing was excellent in Zipolite, but you'd better be careful, extremely careful.

o o o

It happened once that a group from Mexico City was visiting, and noticing that they weren't seaworthy, so to speak, I approached one of the couples to warn them about the dangerous rip tides. They disdainfully dismissed me; I withdrew. A few minutes later, they were desperately fighting a current, which was inexorably pulling them toward a cluster of menacing rocks.

It was Sunday; Zipolite had many visitors from nearby towns, and soldiers were patrolling the beach. The troops, however, were ill-equipped to deal with the situation; they were trying to reach them with ropes, walking over the chain of rocks that descended from the cliff into the ocean.

Usually, all you have to do to get people out of the surf safely is to swim over, calm them down, and guide them away from the current and toward the beach. I had helped a couple of swimmers in distress right in that area.

On this occasion though, the ocean was rather restless, and they were almost upon the rocks. Besides, I didn't have the slightest inclination to risk my life for the louts. I had just warned them!

I sat on the sandy beach to watch the unfolding drama, and when I saw a powerful wave throwing them high against the rocks, I thought with regret that their death was unavoidable; they would be smashed to a pulp by the waves. But somehow, scrambling and clawing in desperation, they secured a hold on the jagged, slippery edges and clambered out. Bruised, cut and bleeding they climbed awkwardly over the sharp rocks, to finally reach the safety of the beach in utter embarrassment but alive.

Perhaps they learned their lesson.

o o o

Gloria's beach was the only not-quite-legal-nude-beach I have seen in Mexico. On weekends, the soldiers would come by to make sure we had our bathing suits on, a good excuse to check the scene. We obligingly put them on.

To body surf, however, I always wore my bathing suit. I felt so vulnerable out there when naked, waiting for the right wave with my equipment floating in the depths amid hungry fish. I shuddered at the thought of a predatory fish mistaking my piece for a juicy new species.

o o o

At times, Gloria's place was a lively place; at times we danced to the beat of drums, under the hot tropical sun, until we dropped. This was part of my experience the first time I stayed at the village. I remember also that travelers and locals alike had a certain awareness about them, and the rapport between all of us was uncanny. Gloria didn't allow drugs or alcohol in the premises, which was a good way to screen the guests and foster a good ambience.

I remember Naomi and Woody, and Franz and Nira, and David and his daughter from British Colombia, and Richard "Bongos" Gringas from Montreal, and Julio, and Pedro el Malo, and Paul and Yvette also from Canada. I remember the Germans and the Spaniards. I remember Gary and his girlfriend Kim from California; their address disappeared in the process of doing laundry and I was never able to visit them in California.

o o o

Oil lamps flickering in the ocean breeze, moving the shadows as they did. A few guests were chatting at the dinning tables.

Nira and I were dancing at Gloria's restaurant. Her husband Franz was playing his drums in a frenzy. Unexpectedly, she sat down and I finished the piece by myself. Then Nira came over and said:

"It took you away, didn't it?"

I looked at her in awe.

"Did you *see* it?"

"Yes I did."

I returned to Zipolite twice, but I never found such people again. Nothing ever repeats.

o o o

But again, I stayed at Gloria's place. Her hammocks and huts had the vantage point of height, and the view during full moon nights could keep you awake.

Gloria lived at the very top of the cliff, where she had built herself a sturdy little log cabin with a loft and a royal view.

The cabin was a round construction with a floor of dirt and a thatched roof.

She was quite a character, Gloria was. American by birth she had become a Mexican citizen by marriage. We had become friends, and I asked her permission to use the meditation room: a little enclosure she had built on sheer cliff at the back of her house. It had no railings for safety, so it had an uninterrupted, spectacular view of nothing but the immense Pacific Ocean and distant ships.

o o o

Not everything was wholesome in Zipolite, of course. I remember a night when I went to the village for dinner—Gloria's cozy restaurant overlooking the beach was always inviting, but sometimes you just feel like eating out. I remember entering one of the thatched restaurants to find a drunk haranguing the patrons. I stopped. Our eyes met, and I saw a mentally unbalanced and quarrelsome young man.

An unfortunate puppy was sniffing the ground at his feet, and to provoke all present the man grabbed one of his hind legs and lifted him up disregarding his anguished yelps. The puppy writhed and squealed hanging helplessly in obviously excruciating pain.

"Want a dog?" the drunk screamed, looking at me while swinging the puppy into more pain.

What could I do? I was disgusted, which was precisely what the drunk wanted. He wanted a reaction from somebody.

The hut was full of patrons and nobody was reacting, which was good. But nobody was acting either. None of the patrons seemed to care. The owners of the place, and probably owners of the dog also, didn't seem to care either. The puppy was still squealing in pain when I forced myself to leave.

I confess that I felt terrible when forsaking that little dog to his fate. But at the time I didn't know what else to do, as the drunkard seemed to be ready to inflict more pain upon intervention; the puppy was practically a hostage. I had also heard, that a village's drunk would fare better than an unknown traveler, when facing the Mexican authorities after an argument; and I was doing business in Mexico with a tourist visa, a situation that placed me in no position to argue. Upset, I trudged into the night toward the sandy beach. I don't remember where I had dinner that night.

Later, with hindsight, I thought that I could have called the soldiers stationed in town. But I don't think they would have cared to intervene either; in Mexico dogs are just dogs. Or I could have rallied everybody to leave the place, for without an audience the show would have stopped. Improbable! I am not that charismatic.

o o o

It also happened at the end of that first stay in Zipolite that I met Cheryl, and we left Zipolite together. I probably should have left her behind; she was a brat at the last minute, in public. But I really liked her, and perhaps I also wanted to spite a couple of the hunks who were after her, so I disregarded her antics.

We didn't travel far though. Nothing like living under one roof to get you to know your girl. Cheryl wanted me to sell her. She didn't say it in so many words. She just said that once she got 100 dollars for "it."

"Easy money," she said.

Cheryl was a stunning beauty, so I figured she sold herself cheap, but I didn't care to be her pimp. We parted company in Taxco; she said she wanted to see some friends in Mexico City. That day as well, I lost my appetite.

o o o

Finally, I made a decision; I would go back to the states and try to publish my manuscript. I would leave my nomadic and stimulating life, selling my own work, for what I knew was coming: odd jobs to support myself while I did what I had to do. On the bus, watching the Pacific Ocean roll by, I promised myself that my stay in the United States would be short; I would soon be south of the border again. I didn't have a clear idea of what I was getting into.

But I guess it's true. Don Juan told Castaneda once, that sometimes you have to be in places and situations you don't like, in order to grow and develop. He actually put Castaneda in such places on purpose; for instance: the mangy hotel in which he (his ego) was supposed to die. Life is a test. It was in the states, I have to admit, where I started developing and realizing.

I crossed the border in Tijuana, and from San Ysidro, I boarded the trolley heading to San Diego, CA where I was to start my new life. It was like entering another world; I had been away for several years and a culture shock awaited.

o o o

San Diego, California is located along the Pacific Ocean. It is a city with beautiful beaches, a tourist attraction. It has within reach snowy mountains and breathtaking desert landscapes, and its average temperature throughout the year is 70° Fahrenheit.

Thus, San Diego is also a spoiled town, a good example of unconscious wealth; it doesn't see its homeless. I heard once a native comedienne refer to the city as "a hick town." But she loved it anyway.

At the onset, I rented a room in an old, shabby and inexpensive hotel south of Broadway—skid row in those days. I secured there a view to the street, to a parade of human misery: from the mentally ill to hardened criminals and prostitutes. I was unwittingly doing what Castaneda had done.

It is intriguing that human beings, supposedly the most intelligent species on the planet, can choose to live in degradation. I hardened in that hotel. By the end of my stay, I didn't care anymore about the stabbings or fights below my window, or in the parking lot located catty-cornered. I didn't have a phone anyway, so there wasn't much I could have done. I just waited for the ambulance to arrive and went back to sleep.

o o o

It was a dangerous place, this area was, where you walked through the acrid smells of human waste emanating from deserted doorways and parking lots; deserted doorways and parking lots sometimes inhabited by homeless people in need of your spare change. I remember going into a restaurant early one night. And as I reached for the doorknob someone grabbed my left arm from behind with an iron grip.

54

I figured the man was close behind me so I swung back with my right elbow at where I thought his face would be. I think I missed him by a strand, for he lost his grip and balance, trying to avoid the blow, and almost fell flat on his ass. I am not a stranger to street violence, and I used to box, so I turned around and faced him.

Rather clumsily, and speaking incoherently, the man took a fighting stand himself; he seemed to be either thoroughly drunk or heavily drugged. As a skinny teenager, growing up in a rather mean neighborhood, and getting my ass kicked occasionally, I learned that if I was going to fight bigger guys and win, I had to hit first and keep hitting until the fight was over—and use whatever was handy. With that training, I was able to win some fights in the army that maybe I should have added to the ones I lost.

At the moment, however, I had no desire to get involved in a street brawl with a drug addict, so I dismissed him as you would any obnoxious jackass who is drunk; I turned around and entered the restaurant. But being bigger than me, I guess he was upset for having almost bitten the dust, and tried to follow me inside. The owner of the place, aware of his intentions, kicked him out.

I had not seen him trying to follow me until I saw the owner, who knew me, blocking his way and ordering him out, threatening him with the police. After the incident, he asked me if I knew the drunkard, but I didn't have a clue who the man was. I had nodded at him civilly a few minutes before, as I approached the restaurant, and I guess he took that as a sign of weakness. Funny! He made an ass of himself.

Yet, it was in that neighborhood, in that hotel, where I did my first volitional *dreaming;* until then, it had been at random. I guess in a place like that it's easy to feel like leaving your body.

That night I startled myself awake when I entered *dreaming* by willing myself to do it the very moment I went to bed. I fell asleep and in a few seconds, on command, I was *dreaming*. I did it twice, although not for long.

o o o

It was also in that neighborhood where I had an epiphany. It happened shortly after I noticed that being employed was not to my liking anymore. I had grown accustomed to an independent life that had allowed me to go just about anywhere I wanted, while making enough money to do so. I had been able to travel at leisure, either by myself or with attractive company, whenever it had been my wish. Consequently, I had developed again quite a sense of self-importance.

It was this sense of self-importance that sometimes made me standoffish. The harsh environment in which I found myself at the moment, somehow also produced outstanding people. I remember Cliff, in particular, a black fellow with remarkable inner balance, a man of goodwill and integrity.

When he was moving out with his new girl friend, he invited me over for lunch. I never went. I felt patronized, and I refused his friendship due to a false sense of self-reliance.

Breaking away from my past and becoming a rolling stone had helped me to reduce it at first, but indeed, self-importance is a monster with three thousand heads. As we battle the monster and cut a head off, we can't lower our guard, for soon, there will be another head staring at us, jaws open and ready to devour us.

Having done well in my nomadic, independent lifestyle had caused my self-importance to surface again, and it was distorting my perspective. Therefore, after working for a while, helping in construction sites for a temporary agency, I started getting fed up with the low wages and the grueling, meaningless toil. I almost threw my manuscript away and went back to Mexico; it crossed my mind to burn it.

But one day, when passing by a bookstore, I saw a title that grabbed my attention; it made me aware of who my real enemy was. Its title: *The Enemy Within.*

In San Diego I had come across J.R.R. Tolkien's books, *The Hobbit* and *The Lord of the Rings* trilogy, and I had made an analogy. I saw our materialistic way of life as the Balrog, the demon that the sorcerer Gandalf fought over the abyss. Our warped belief system, our money culture, was the Balrog I had to fight and conquer. But when I saw that title a realization struck me like a flash of lightning; I *saw* that the Balrog was also *me.*

The Enemy Within was just a thriller about spies, but I had recently read *The Fire From Within* by Castaneda, and I realized that it was the enemy within, my self-importance, who was encouraging me to leave my trip unfinished and my goal forgotten. The Balrog was indeed the monster with three thousand heads.

The Balrog was *me,* the false *I,* the enemy within. And I resolved to stay and get it done somehow. I decided to learn how to play with the petty tyrants of the world and reduce my ego. As a first step, I trimmed my hair, shaved my beard and mustache (the maid said I looked younger), and started looking for a regular job.

o o o

Petty tyrants, in Castaneda's lingo, are people (usually in positions of power) who are cruel and despotic; they are commonly referred to as assholes. They can have the power of life and death over you, or they can simply be obnoxious enough to try your patience to the limit; the latter are called itsy-bitsy, teeny-weeny petty tyrants.

Don't laugh! According to don Juan, they are the best tool a warrior has at his disposal to get rid of his self-importance; they are, in truth, precious. They are also a source of joy, providing he uses the four attributes of the warrior: control, discipline, forbearance and timing.

Meanwhile (without hate or malice) the warrior maps the tyrant's weaknesses and develops a strategy to deal with him or her. In this manner the warrior is not a victim anymore, and he can apply pressure and enjoy the encounter (sometimes he enjoys himself immensely). The Spirit will eventually guide him to an exit or dispose of the tyrant.

And so it happened that in San Diego, I started to handle petty tyrants with control, discipline, forbearance and timing. When I moved from that hotel south of Broadway, I rented a room in North Park, and I assure you that I had better company at the hotel; this in spite of the fact that Gollum,[†] or someone remarkably similar, lived there. There was also a mentally ill person who, at times, would smear the common toilets and bathrooms with his excrement during the dead of night. And a close by neighbor would lie in bed, in tight briefs, and smile coyly at passersby through the wide open door.

My new roommate and landlady, however, turned out to be a blonde beauty who was also a spoiled itsy-bitsy, teeny-weeny, and superb petty tyrant. She would nag. She would complain. She was excellent at snide remarks. In short, as a petty tyrant, she was outstanding! She even told me once that in her house I had "no rights whatsoever," giving me the perfect *timing* to give notice.

For the duration of my stay, however, I used control, discipline, forbearance and *timing*; I was ruthless, cunning, patient and sweet. It worked! She couldn't rattle me. Baffled, she would hide from me. She would hide because I would greet her smiling from ear to ear saying:

"Hi KG, long time no see, how are you?"

How could I be so amicable when she was being such a bitch? Not once did I lose my temper or composure. I was fighting my self-importance, and that was all that mattered. I had my strategy.

When the fiend was rattling dishes, pots and pans at 5 o'clock in the morning (the kitchen was next to my room) I was already up and doing Yoga. Part of my strategy was to go to bed at the same time she did (although my schedule didn't require it) so that I could get enough sleep in spite of her. And I was always so polite, so friendly. I always had a smile for her.

I will always be in her debt, for she helped me to develop a new perspective, a new outlook on life. I have to admit, however, that at the time I felt no sympathy for the woman. I hadn't understood yet that human beings live in a daze; we have a distorted view of reality due to our ego and its unrelenting self-reflection. We don't see things the way they are; we don't see that everything is interconnected.

[†] A main, evil, grotesque character in *The Lord of the Rings* and *The Hobbit* by JRR Tolkien

o o o

Months after I moved out, I saw KG at Horton Plaza's food court. She was dressed to kill, looking her best. Gorgeous! She recognized me as she passed by, and smiled. I greeted her politely. As she secured a table for herself, I thought that her smile had obviously been inviting, but, I passed. Her beauty was skin deep, and I knew.

Chapter 4

The Venom in the Fog

One ring to rule them all . . .
—The Lord of the Rings, J.R.R. Tolkien

When you are living in darkness, why don't you look for light?
—Buddha

Stalking is a Toltec technique with many ramifications. *Stalking* is what we do when we deal with petty tyrants: We act; we don't react. We develop a strategy to deal with any specific situation, so that we are never victims or tyrants ourselves. *Stalking* is *controlled folly,* being aware that the *dreamed dreams* the *dreamer,* but still playing our part in the world with integrity, breaking away from a faulty social contract while still using it.

Stalking ourselves means we are tactful when we speak, we are aware of our thoughts and emotions; it means we consider death an advisor and reduce our self-importance; it means we are detached while enjoying the pressure of the moment. *Stalking* ourselves is always doing our best.

A master *stalker* is the *impeccable* warrior; he is the illumined man of the Paramahamsa Upanishad: "He praises nobody, blames nobody. He has no need to repeat the mantra, no more need to practice meditation." In other words, he is in constant meditation, always reining the mind and leading it to the present moment. Stalking is what the Buddha calls *mind-*

fulness, and what our grandmothers meant when they said: "You can't cross the bridge until you get to the river." *Stalking* helps you realize how the ego turns into a parasite to become your worst enemy; it will help you break free from the habit of compulsive thinking.

o o o

In San Diego, I started *stalking* myself, and not only I was using my *stalking* strategies with individual petty tyrants, as aforementioned, but also with groups of petty tyrants in companies I worked for. Self-importance was out of the question. I was not trying to chastise people but merely keeping them from making me a victim; they were really my helpers in my fight against egomania. The results were astounding: Nothing bothered me much, and I had a control over me and over extraneous situations that under ordinary circumstances, with my ego at the helm, would have been unattainable.

While working in San Diego, however, my manuscript suffered untold number of rejections. I received a few letters, which acknowledged the merits of the work, but no acceptance. And having been out of the country for a few years, I had no credit or credit cards; neither banks nor private companies would lend me the money I needed to buy a car. So when my mail brought an invitation to visit friends in Canada, the road looked inviting once more.

o o o

Strolling in sunshine down Broadway Avenue toward the bay, I reveled in the cool, stimulating morning. Soft breezes whispered in my ear, and when I smelled the sea in their breath, I longed for the city as if I was already gone. And I remembered Judith.

I had met Judith in San Diego years before. I was still living in Mexico at the time but I crossed the border to comply with Mexican laws, sell my crafts and Mexican imports, and stay briefly with friends whom I had met in Mexico. It was Friday night when my friend Tatty invited Judith over to meet me, a blind date, sort off.

I opened the door for Judith to be duly impressed. She was enthralling in her simplicity, a dazzling smile. I was able to keep my composure and invite her in smoothly. And we met, and we all chatted while relaxing in the Jacuzzi. There was a connection!

But as Judith and I were going out, Tatty decided to join us. I stood aghast, for her boyfriend William was finishing a work project and he couldn't go anywhere. The number 3 has never looked as repulsive as it did that night, but there was nothing I could do; I was the guest.

Our connection, however, survived the outing, and Judith and I decided to have lunch together on Sunday—a real date; not everything was lost. I promised to call her that Sunday morning at 11 o'clock.

And I did, but she wasn't home. Her roommate was kind enough to take a message and jot down my new address, at the downtown YMCA, and my phone number. Then I waited, and waited, and waited. Nothing!

I went for a stroll along Balboa Park to clear my head. And I admit to a feeling of utter desolation; for me, it had been love at first sight.

Two days later, I called Tatty and William to thank them for their hospitality, and Tatty explained that Judith had called me on Sunday, but she didn't know my last name. And the front desk clerk, who didn't know my nickname, had told her that I wasn't registered there and refused to connect her to my room.

I didn't call her again. I am sure the ego must have been involved, rearing one of its ugly heads.

I was disappointed. She had not been there for me. In her place, I would have done my best to find her, so either she wasn't spunky enough or she wasn't really interested. A few weeks later, I sent a letter to Tatty from Chiapas, Mexico, trying to explain, but I never received an answer and somehow all connections were lost.

And Judith vanished, as a dream would, as we all will. And probably she will never know, but I still wonder at times what would have happened if . . .

Is there such a thing as fate?

And now the road beckoned again, with promises galore. And *again*, I left. Does it really matter?

o   o   o

I'll call her Sally. I met her in the train, in the lounge car; she was running away with her three kids. Sally was escaping the cruelty and abuse of her ex-husband, and she was afraid. She figured he would find them eventually. But she didn't know what else to do. Sally said restraining orders had proved useless.

Her words poured out. I didn't know what to say. Somebody said something.

Years later, I found a book in which a Buddhist teacher was discussing the topic of killing. He said that to kill or not to kill was not the question; the question was, why did you kill? Isn't that true? To protect yourself, or your family, it might be your duty to kill.

I wonder about Sally's fate sometimes.

o o o

Radium Hot Springs is an alluring mountain village. It flaunts the world famous Radium Hot Springs Mineral Pools and some of the most beautiful alpine scenery I have ever seen. A spring is born in the mountains that border my friends' ranch, and it provides fresh water for all their needs.

Their guesthouse was in the corral, and Paul's sleek black mare would come to greet me every morning, making the place a home. I was tempted to mount her once, for she was also a gentle being. It would have been easy from the sun deck, which was her height. But it was good that I didn't, my hosts explained later, for the horse had not been ridden for some time, and she could have thrown me off.

o o o

It was Ivette, who understands clearly the human predicament, who made me aware of a critical fact. We were chatting in the huge tee pee they had pitched not far from their comfortable log house: a fairly large house they had built with their own hands, amid a forest of commanding ponderosa pines. And she said that if I felt vexed about not being able to control my self-reflection, my ego was back at work and I was missing the point.

Alas! Vexation is ego stuff; in anger or anxiety there is the ego at work. The mystic, San Juan de la Cruz said: "Disquietude is always vanity, because it serves no good. Even if the whole world were thrown into confusion and all things in it, disquietude on that account would be vanity."

o o o

Ivette has no fear of the bears that may stray onto the neighborhood. She even talks to them if she finds them around the yard. Thus, I still worry about her at times, for bears can be moody and unpredictable; they are liable to attack, and either kill you or change your façade for no apparent reason.

They are also, I admit, a good source of protein. Our dinner one night was bear steaks, and mine was delicious. Paul told me that when the bear is older, the meat is softened by hanging the carcass and letting it decompose briefly, before it is cleaned and placed in the freezer.

I guess we can't complain if bears think that we are ourselves a good source of protein sometimes. What can we say?

o o o

It was springtime, and the pungent aroma of the imposing ponderosa pines lingered in the air; along the countryside flowers bloomed in sunshine, enjoying the warm morning and the song of myriad birds. During a sparkling day as such we visited the hot springs.

But everything is impermanent in this world of time, and my visit also had to end. Yvette took me to Banff, in the near state of Alberta, where we hugged in farewell. She wanted me to see the Rocky Mountain's historic town, and ride its gondola to the summit of Sulphur Mountain for the spectacular view.

And although it was the month of May, it snowed in Banff while I was there.

o o o

I stayed in Seattle.

The world famous Pike Street Market is in Seattle, and it has a fish market where employees are really skilled at catching fish; and mind you, they put some muscle in that pitch. It is a show! Those guys are having fun. Their customers can join the catch-and-toss as well, but whether they do or not they thoroughly enjoy the show, and that fish market does really quite well.

It rains in Seattle, but I don't think it's quite as much as it is said. And during the sunny warm days of summer, I used to swim in Lake Washington at Madison Park.

Only once, during January, I saw Seattle snowed in for quite a wintry week. I can't remember the year. Chaos ensued, for the city is lacking in snow plows, and shoveling icy sidewalks is not a people's skill in Seattle. Ditched cars (and people) were a common sight that week.

I stayed in Seattle because I had heard that it had a reputable dance community (the city is a major cultural and educational center) and, while living in San Diego, I had started taking dance lessons. I love dancing; it is an excellent way to keep in shape. It is also a way to touch the Spirit: there is dance and . . . *dance.*

What triggered my decision to take classes was an experience I had in a nightclub. There was fine music at the place and an acceptable dance floor. So, while in the process of drinking my beer, I asked three ladies (in different rounds, of course) if they'd dance. All of them had these incredible looking legs, so I figured they could move. As if with one accord they all said:

"No thank you, maybe later."

Have you ever gotten that response?

I finished my beer. I went out. And while looking at the stars upon the clear San Diego sky, I decided to get trained so that I could dance on my own at nightclubs and still look good.

Next day, I went to a downtown studio called Stage 7, on Seventh Avenue, close to Broadway, where I got introduced to jazz dance. I had been mistaken about jazz; it is a very athletic form of dance. Jazz dance (in case you don't know) is what Travolta did in *Saturday Night Fever* and Jennifer Beal (or her double) did in *Flashdance*; it is Bob Fosse's dance—theater dance.

When in my ignorance I told the artistic director that I just wanted to learn a few steps and perform, she looked at me as if I was completely nuts. And after explaining that I had to train if I wanted to hold an audience, she suggested that I should take a class to see what I thought.

Although holding an audience was not exactly what I had in mind, I did take the class. And I was hooked! I performed my first choreographed piece less than a year later in Balboa Park, wrecking my shoes and my ankles in the process. I had to wear ankle braces for a couple of weeks, and I didn't make enough tips to buy them. What the hell, I was a beginner.

Due to being a beginner and my choreography and style needing improvement, I was getting strong reactions from the public. It was a stimulating experience. I remember that as a young couple went by during that park performance, the woman made a snide remark:

"You are not taking yourself seriously, are you?"

I was taken aback by the vile in her tone but did not falter. After finishing the performance, and while talking to a lady who apparently had enjoyed the piece, the couple again sauntered by and I caught another snide remark.

I can't remember what I responded. I was trying to figure out what was bothering her, but she did not seem to know herself. Disdainfully, she kept walking; her boyfriend was unconcerned. Was her problem envy? The ego at work? I was having fun!

o o o

Becoming a dancer not only enriched my new life, it was like becoming somebody else; it was something completely different from what I had ever done. I don't have family in show business, and was not raised dancing professionally.

Where I grew up we did dance, and some of us, I am sure, were the precursors of the break dancers of today. But going to a dance school was something that only girls did. It wouldn't even have crossed my mind to take a dance class then. In Seattle, I started with Jazz at Madrona dance school, the Jessup/Jenkins dance studio, and Dance Center Seattle. Then I studied ballet with Pacific Northwest Ballet.

In Seattle I also tried to make a living as a portrait artist for a while—another skill I had learned and polished in San Diego before I started dancing. I worked on the long, winding, wide stairs that climbed down from the Pike Street Market to the piers. I remember I also sold a few of my pastels. But just like in San Diego's Balboa Park, my income was meager, so I decided I had to go back to work.

In Seattle, however, I was able to establish credit and get a credit card. So after working as a sales clerk with a jewelry store for a couple of years, I decided to buy a car through a friend's connection. I bought a new turquoise-blue Plymouth Colt, a hatchback, to try my luck elsewhere.

By *elsewhere*, I mean a sales job that had been secured for me by friends: Associates I had met at a network marketing company in which we all failed to achieve anything. It was a sales job that also turned sour due to unreliable and dishonest management.

In the meantime my effort to reduce my self-importance continued, and I was gaining ground. To save my new car and myself, I took a job with a national pizza delivery company. That job turned out to be extremely helpful; they had a great manual on safe driving while delivering a pizza in 30 minutes or less. I became a much better driver.

The job also gave me a steady income, and produced a flow of petty tyrants in streaming succession, forcing me to new heights of personal growth. I had to develop complex strategies to deal with an unlimited amount of conceited idiots in positions of power, and avoid being a victim or losing my control.

It required transformation; a transformation that was due. Do you remember that I used to get fired from restaurants etcetera? Not anymore! I kept my control and discipline with forbearance; the timing to turn the tables on the petty tyrants was always there.

But of course, I know you understand that to break free from the chains imposed by the ego is no mean feat; the monster with three thousand heads wants to feed itself, and it is relentless. Every day the challenge starts anew.

o   o   o

I knocked on the door to hear an old voice asking if I was the pizza man. I identified myself and she said that she was on a wheelchair to please open the door.

I was in the Central District, one of the worst parts of town. I opened the door to see a revolver pointed straight at me; the lady *was* on a wheelchair. I asked her what was going on. She said it was Friday night and she couldn't take chances; *they* could break into her house anytime. *They* steal to buy drugs. On weekends, she stays awake, gun in hand. *They* know she is alone.

The place was an old, decrepit and poorly lit shack, impossible to secure. Her position was untenable, the scene surreal!

I placed her pizza on a nearby table where there was a twenty-dollar bill. I placed the change right next to the pizza. I was speechless. She bid me good night.

In such places sometimes the customers tip; in such places sometimes the pizza gets stolen or the driver mugged.

Does anything makes sense?

o o o

Toltecs claim knowledge only if they can act on it. Isn't that a sound principle? The Buddha Himself prompts us to verify:

"Do not believe anything you read or hear," Buddha states (not even what He Himself says), "until you have experienced its truth."

While *stalking* myself, I verified that our constant self-reflection is our major weakness. Self-importance was definitely the major weakness of the petty tyrants I was dealing with; their buttons, I realized, were so easily pushed. Upon close examination, you can also see the strong connection existing between stupidity and self-importance; they are an inseparable couple, a marriage made in hell. As a consequence, the most intelligent species in this world (supposedly) is also the most cruel, vindictive and destructive.

A dense fog, which practically annuls our intelligence, oozes from our obsessive egomania turning us into an immoral and obtuse species. There is venom in this fog. A venom that breeds anger, hate and greed. We create enemies where none exist. In our folly, we make our past mistakes an intolerable burden to be carried for life, and worry about a future that will never come.

We forgo the present moment, and consequently, don't see things the way they really are. It is the Christ* who says that the man who takes to the plow and looks back is not worthy of the Kingdom of Heaven, and that by worrying about the future you can't add a single hour to your life. ... "tomorrow will take care of itself."† These are strong statements referring to the importance of presence.

Using our past for reference is essential; living in it is absurd. Making plans for the future is necessary, worrying about an imaginary future, or expecting fulfillment from it is madness; until it is here, the future does not exist, and what happens *now* can either change your plans or cancel them altogether.

o o o

My main manager at the moment (in a department store) is a blind egomaniac, a complete jackass, and one of the best itsy-bitsy, teeny-weeny petty tyrants I've ever had. She was disrespectful and insolent. I did not react. I am not angry. I know the parasite owns her; the ego is running and ruining her life.

But being a victim is out of the question, for I would lose my balance and well being—an untenable position. So I make an appointment with her to explain that disrespectful behavior is not only against company policy, it is not acceptable.

That appointment is a week from now. Today I plan my moves for that day, what I will say and how, to stop her unconscious behavior. After my plans are laid the subject is closed until the set date. I will not allow my mind to worry about an outcome that I can't foretell; I will not review what I am going to say anymore until the time comes. I will stay in the present moment, for after having planned strategically

---

* Gospel of Luke (9:62)
† Gospel of Mathew (6:25)

the consequences of our meeting are irrelevant. The Spirit will decide the outcome.

This, I admit, is not easy to do; it does take, in Buddha's lingo, the right effort, for you are breaking the lifelong habit of reinforcing your ego by talking to yourself. But it is doable. If the coming event is overpowering, count to 8 repeatedly and *just do your best. Stalk* yourself: be aware of what your mind is doing—working against *you*. And remember, you can't cross the bridge until you reach the river.

o o o

To be present is our most pressing challenge, a challenge that we choose to ignore. And I say *choose* because most of us, at one time or another during our lives, realize that something is out of kilter, but we don't care to make an effort to discover what. We decide to put the matter aside, for it seems too much trouble to search, find what's wrong, and take action; it is easier to accept the status quo.

At that precise moment we are willingly sacrificing our depth to remain in delusion; we are turning our backs on the Source. From that moment on we are responsible for our ignorance. And individually and collectively we will have to face the consequences, for we always reap what we sow.

o o o

My niece sent me an email once with the following subject: *They are dying.* She was referring to words. Her language teacher had told her that words were loosing their meaning due to misuse and abuse. I answered that it was true; her teacher was right. And as an example I told her that I don't use the word *God* anymore, for it is so widely misused that it has lost its meaning; it is mostly used to justify our misdeeds.

It seems that our idea of God is just a projection of our ego; our Gods have been created after our image and likeness.

"We are the center of creation," we say. "We are made after the image and likeness of God," we repeat.

And, of course, our God is always better than *their* God, so we kill and destroy in the name of our Gods.

It is more likely that the Being who resides in everything does not have an image or likeness to anything in particular. *It* reflects everything equally. *It* is totally incomprehensible to our reason, and we ourselves are part of *It*. Lift a rock and there you'll find me, cut a piece of wood and in the splinters you shall also find me; isn't that what the Christ said?

But for us to *see* this we need to reduce the ego; that is, we need inner silence. The reasoning mind can't pierce the fog; it creates the fog. Prayer misses the point; it implies that we are separate from the Source. We aren't! That is delusion. And that is why the Christ ‡ says: "Pray, and you we shall be condemned."

Silence!

"Be still and know that I am God."—Psalms 46:10

o o o

"Are you looking for me? I am in the next seat.
My shoulder is against yours.
You will not find me in Stupas, not in Indian Shrine rooms,
Nor in Synagogues, nor in Cathedrals,
Not in masses, nor chants,
Not in legs winding around your own neck.
Nor in eating nothing but vegetables.
When you really look for me, you will see me instantly.
You will find me in the tiniest house of time.
Kabir says: Students tell me what is God?
He is the breath inside the breath."—Kabir

o o o

There is a story about three Christian monks who lived as hermits in a small island. Their bishop, who was living in the mainland, heard that their prayer consisted of the following:

"We are three, thou are three, please have mercy."

Upon learning this, His Highness decided to go and teach them how to pray properly. He traveled to the island, and the three monks, who were thoroughly excited with his visit, agreed to learn how to pray.

---

‡ Gospel of Thomas (14a)

When the bishop was leaving, however, he saw an intense light following the boat. As the light approached he saw that it was the three monks running to overtake the boat. When they did, one of them asked His Highness to please teach them the prayers one more time because they had forgotten them. The bishop looked at them hovering over the water and humbly told them that they should keep praying as they have been.

Ramana Maharshi said that the degree of absence of thought is the measure of progress in self-realization.

o o o

Adolph Hitler was an extreme case of egomania; he wanted to make the world after his image and likeness. We could say that in Hitler and his accomplices' case the venom was quite potent; theirs was a case of extreme self-importance, an acute egomania that would justify heinous crimes and extreme cruelty.

A documentary film, which I saw at the University of Arizona once, showed a witness in a film about the Nuremberg trials, who, while passing by the defendants on the way to testify, looked at them briefly. She declared in the documentary that she had looked at them, wondering about their appearance since they had to be monsters; after all, she had been a witness to a horrifying crime: One night, children had been thrown into the ovens alive because the gas chambers had malfunctioned.

They didn't look like monsters, however, they looked like normal human beings. And I am sure they were normal human beings. Normal human beings who overwhelmed by the fog and its venom developed a hideous psyche.

o o o

On a minor scale, we can see this warped behavior everywhere. We are all afflicted with it.

At the moment, I am looking at the label on a can of Chicken and Dumplings that I bought about a month ago. It reads: "Homestyle Goodness." It can't be! There can't be any homestyle goodness in canned food.

There can't be any freshness in food that has been frozen, but it will still be sold as fresh food in every supermarket on a regular basis. And this is the way human beings deal with each other continuously. We are predators to our own species in every conceivable way; try getting an honest mechanic. It will take you a while.

One of the few honest ads I have come across, I found in a restaurant in Las Cruces, New Mexico. It read:

"If you want a home cooked dinner, go home!"

But this is rather unusual.

Yet, human beings take a society plagued by dishonesty and corruption as normal. Obviously, for us to consider this behavior normal, our psyche must have been warped by centuries of living within this fog produced by our egomania. How could it be otherwise?

About that can of Chicken and Dumplings that I just mentioned, well, I opened it. I found many dumplings and traces of chicken. I dumped most of the dumplings; I figured it was for the better. I couldn't find any "Homestyle Goodness" at all . . . at all.

o o o

During one of my stays in California, I was walking one morning toward the laundry room in my apartment complex. A little girl, perhaps five years old, was standing on the lawn beside the walkway. As I approached I waved and said, "Hi!" She was so beautiful and looked so bright. The charming little girl waved as I passed by, giving me the sweetest smile while whispering:

"I can't talk! . . . I can't talk!"

She didn't fully understand why she couldn't talk; she was talking to me. But I knew what she meant. She had been admonished against talking to strangers due to the risks involved in such an act. I had no intention of stopping, and as I kept walking I waved good-bye while nodding to let her know that I understood: Human beings prey even on their own children.

Is this normal behavior for an intelligent species?

o o o

In the prologue to one of his books, I read that J.R.R. Tolkien stated in an interview, that there was no allegory behind his work; his only purpose was to entertain. Perhaps he was teasing his interviewer; or, if he meant it, human beings are undoubtedly subliminally conscious of our predicament.

In Tolkien's trilogy: *The Lord of the Rings,* good triumphs over evil; the main characters conquer the passions fostered by the evil ring of Sauron to finally destroy it—almost failing at the end. The sorcerer Gandalf, Frodo, Bilbo, and select company transcend their physical form and leave the world in a grand finale.

In our world, however, the triumph of humanity over the passions fostered by an unruly ego is yet to come. The *first ring of power* rules the earth; the world of the senses casts a veil to hide the interconnectedness of everything, creating a world of separation in which the ego rules. Consequently, we live in darkness and corruption; our egotism breeds a world in which divisiveness, fear, greed and cruelty prevail.

"One ring to rule them all. One ring to find them. One ring to bring them all and in the darkness bind them."

I tend to think that in the aforementioned interview professor Tolkien was humoring us.

o o o

In Seattle, I became a publisher.

After receiving positive comments from a few publishing companies, but still no acceptance, I did some research, and I came to the conclusion that it was better to publish the manuscript myself. I learned that unless publishers give you an advance (and as a rule this only happens if you are a celebrity or a famous author) they don't really do much for your book.

They also own the book, and usually you don't have a saying on the cover art. I decided to do it myself and get it over with. Time was of the essence.

Hence, when the book was published in August of 1993, I expected it to be a flop. A book published by a regular publisher has a crucial advantage: many qualified editors. I had one, whom I had to correct at times.

I almost wished it to be a flop. Writing is hard work with usually low pay, if any, and I knew that I was fighting against all odds. Thus, I thought, if my readers decide that I am not good, so be it! I will surrender my pen.

Imagine! I would have been free to just travel and dance.

As chance would have it, however, a neighbor recommended the book buyer for The Elliot Bay Book Company (in Pioneer Square) as an intelligent man who knew books; he would give me an honest opinion. I left him a copy, which he perused for about a week, and he ordered ten more.

The book was good, he said. And I was hooked.

He also advised me to get a distributor, because most bookstores only bought through them. I followed his advice and signed a contract with Pacific Pipeline, a small distributor. Soon after, I secured my first favorable review in a small newspaper: The Northwest Ethnic News.

o o o

The first book signing I did in Seattle was successful. The owner of The Second Story Bookstore in Wallingford was impressed. Moreover, The Elliott Bay Book Company was not only carrying my book but also selling it.

And shortly after that first book signing, Waldenbooks accepted my book through another intelligent book buyer, and I started doing book signings for them at different locations. *A Vagabond in Mexico* was selling by word of mouth; it was selling because of its merits, no hype!

The postman brought me a thank you card from a school teacher in northern Washington. After reading *A Vagabond in Mexico*, she said, the plight of illegal immigrants was obvious. And Carl Franz the author of *The People's Guide to Mexico* contacted me requesting a copy to do another review; someone had brought the book to his attention.

A promotional tour was unavoidable.

Chapter 5

Detachment

It is no measure of health to be well adjusted to a profoundly sick society.—J. Krishnamurti

When you are on a journey of awareness, you are on a journey on your own; you don't have the buffer of friends and relatives, or any social status. You are deprogramming your mind. You are breaking boundaries.

Thus, it was occurring: I was becoming invisible. Although not obviously so at the beginning, it was occurring.

In Toltec folklore, the main reason to drop your personal history is to reduce your self-importance, to reduce the *I*. But when you start loosing your self-importance, you also start breaking away from a global social contract, for self-importance is a basic element in most societies in the world today. It is hard to relate to you when you do not have any importance due to lacking points of reference; you have begun to walk the edge of the razor; you are indeed becoming invisible.

o o o

When I started to drop my personal history, I unknowingly started a process conducing to my symbolic death; that is, the death of the ego. Since, in truth, in the world of matter the ego is necessary, to "kill the ego" has to be considered a figure of speech; the ego must be seen for what it is, a mental fabrication, a character in a play, a point of reference, so it will not hold the baton anymore.

In this respect Seattle was of great help to me in many ways, for it was in Seattle that middle age caught me. It was as if I had crossed a dividing line of some sort, and suddenly I was a middle-aged man.

It happened that I was walking down Spring Street one day, on my way to work, when suddenly I saw a reflection in a store window. And there it was, staring right at me. I recoiled, but there was no escape; it pounced upon me and snatched my youth. I became a middle-aged man.

A middle-aged man who apparently had forgotten to change his nomadic lifestyle and settle down, who had refused to forget his search and join mainstream America. When middle age sneaked up on me it made me more of an outsider. It made Seattle hostile.

o o o

Paradoxically, my body didn't feel middle age at all, for by then I was an advanced dancer and performer, dancing four and five days a week. I was in the best physical shape I have ever been in.

Even so, after my book was published, only a few of my dance peers cared to take a look or buy it. And some, who I had thought to be my friends, would go as far as to blatantly sidestep or avoid my book signings.

It was a rather peculiar behavior:

There was J____ at Bumbershoot's* Book fair. She stood a few feet from my booth.

"Hi!" I said upon recognition, while pointing to my books.

"Do you work here?" she replied without moving, although we had talked about my manuscript.

"No" I shook my head. "This is my book . . . remember?"

"Oh!"

And saying no more she spun on her heels and disappeared, merging with the bustling crowd.

---

* Bumbershoot is an annual international music and art festival.

At the mall, in Waldenbooks, it had been total avoidance. Coming toward me was T____. Strange was her behavior: My jutting table was unavoidable; she saw me across the aisle; she vanished.

Women of straw! Was it envy? It was incomprehensible.

Did I make a mistake not returning to California? Stage 7 was, by far, a better school than most, and there was also Edge in Los Angeles. Dogen Zenji, a renowned Zen Master, said once that the life of a Zen Master is one continuous mistake. Alas, I have something in common with the masters.

But as I mentioned before, uncomfortable places or adverse situations are an aid in disguise, if you use them to your advantage. Seattle's dancers helped me to understand better the net that entangles the programmed mind, the pettiness of an ego-driven society.

I also understood that what made me a dancer was neither praise nor my insuperable technique or athleticism (I had neither of them), but the fact that I could become the *dance*. I still remember my graduation night, so to speak.

I was doing a solo performance in a two day show at Dance Center Seattle. On Saturday, our first night, we had quite a receptive audience, but somehow, dancing a piece that I had rehearsed and perfected for months, I was a little off at the end. I went home determined to figure out where the problem was. I worked until about 4 o'clock in the morning, and finally solved the riddle.

I got up about 7 o'clock (I can never sleep late after being up all night), ate breakfast and went back to bed. After quieting my mind (I had an exciting day ahead), I managed to sleep until noon and recover my lost sleep. I was ready for the night's show.

After a good lunch I went to the Dance Center and prepared for the show to the best of my ability. That night I *danced*. It was my own choreography to Michael Jackson's *Bad,* and I remember thinking while flying in a jump:

"This could be illegal."

In the words of J___ H___ one of my teachers:

"You get into it."

○ ○ ○

Daniel Nagrin once complained to his wife Helen Tamiris (both famous Broadway dancers) about his peers' snide remarks as he rehearsed that extra half hour. She responded: "Daniel you are like a thorn on their side; they resent you."

It is noteworthy that Mr. Nagrin's training and his book, *How to Dance Forever* seemed to have been partly influenced by Castaneda's work—Castaneda is one of his references. And Daniel explains how dancers are frequently crippled by the ego; one of his colleagues calls it: "ego-static." We judge ourselves and other dancers instead of paying attention to the steps and movements that we are learning, and we hinder ourselves.

To Daniel's book I owe my pre-performance ritual: On performance days, I always do my pieces at least three times before the show, twice during the morning and once as close to my appearance on stage as I can, so that during that evening's show I will not be doing a "first" dance, which is the hardest.

Daniel's advice to start warming up ten to fifteen minutes before one's turn to go on stage proved particularly helpful; I jogged in place; I did push ups, kicks, jumps, stretches . . . you name it, while other dancers looked on as if I was crazy. But by the time it was my turn to go on stage, I was sweating, and that gave me an edge; I was fully warm and ready to go. After the last group performance I did in school, even my teacher paid me a compliment, and he seldom spoke to me.

By then, however, I was beginning to master detachment. I had understood that the psyche of man has been warped for millenniums by the ego, and the fog and its venom prevails. So approval or disapproval by my fellow humans was irrelevant. I was breaking free from a distorted social contract; I had an abstract purpose.

In Toltec lore, I was looking for new lodgings. And I had to do what I had to do without fear of failure or hope for success, enjoy the action free from expectations.

Detachment, by the way, never means that we do not care about anything or anybody; it means rather that we accept the fact that everything is interconnected and helping others is helping ourselves. We *detach* from the ego to *see* the Whole.

o o o

There was a fellow dancer in Seattle, who died of AIDS. He came to class until the very end, and his emaciated condition was a telltale sign.

This young man would not give me the time of day to his last dying day. And so I learned that homosexuals (not all of them, I admit) can be as intolerant as heterosexuals, and ruthless in their rejection. In their opinion, we are not supposed to be on the dance floor.

o o o

When the words of the Bhagavad Gita, the most profound and influential of the Hindu Scriptures, are given to him, the warrior Arjuna is about to engage in battle. Eighteen armies will fight eighteen days and nights almost to the last man, sacrificing their integrity in the process. It will be Armageddon, the climatic battle of the Mahabharata.[†]

Although Arjuna is the best warrior on the battlefield and fighting for a just cause, he is greatly disheartened; for to restore the throne to his brother he will be fighting his own cousins and former teachers. Before the battle, while surveying the battlefield, Arjuna tosses his weapons to the ground in despair, and addressing the god Krishna, who is disguised as his charioteer, he asks for guidance:

"How does a warrior perform his duty without doing wrong, polluting himself with the blood of his enemy?"

"The secret is detachment," answers Krishna.[‡] "Do your duties without concern for personal consequences. Victory and defeat, pleasure and pain are all the same. Act but don't reflect on the fruits of the act. Forget desire, seek detachment. Fight! But stay free from the fever of the ego."

The goal of action is knowledge of the Spirit, but it must be selfless action. This means that the real conflict is with the ego-self, on the battlefield of the psyche.

[†] The Mahabharata has been called "a literature in itself," and it is said that, "if it is not in the Mahabharata, it is not anywhere else." It is an epic of immense proportions, comparable in depth and scope to the whole of Greek literature or Shakespeare.

[‡] Baghavad Gita 3:30

"Actions do not cling to me because I am not attached to their results"—Krishna.

o o o

Our spiritual growth is not stunted by pleasurable or painful experiences, but by selfish attachment or aversion to them. It is the mental state created by the experience that is all-important.

In an old Zen story two monks marching along a river see a woman who has no means to cross. To help her, the senior monk carries her over to the other side. The story does not say what happened across the river. Who knows? She could have been a seductress. But on the way to the monastery his partner is so obsessed by the event that he can talk of nothing else.

"A monk is not supposed to touch a woman," he keeps saying, "let alone carry her in his arms. What have you done?"

Finally the senior monk puts an end to it.

"I left that woman on the bank," he retorts. "You are still carrying her."

Indeed, without the emotional charge the experience itself is insignificant. We need to face pleasure and pain, success and failure, praise and blame with detachment and equanimity. "The awakened sages call a person wise when all his undertakings are free from anxiety about results. All his selfish desires have been consumed in the fire of knowledge. The wise, ever satisfied, have abandoned all external supports. Their security is unaffected by the results of their action; even while acting, they really do nothing at all. Free from expectations and from all sense of possession, with mind and body firmly controlled by the Self, they do not incur sin by the performance of physical action." §

o o o

Detachment is also a key factor in the sexual act. In Tantra Yoga sex is performed in a way that helps the practitioner to awake. There is no selfishness or possessiveness in the

---

§ Bhagavad Gita (4-19 to 21)

act, no manipulation or neediness, no clinging. Selfless involvement and unconditional love are the essential requirements. It is said to be one of the fastest ways to drop the ego and awake.

One of the goals of Tantra is for the lovers to transcend their individuality and become one, to then unite with the Absolute. "…for the ultimate goal of the practice is to descend from the non-dual experience better equipped to experience the multiplicity of the world without estrangement." **

Why should sex be feared or rejected? It is essential to life and a great pleasure. It is the mystic and poet Kabir who says in rather prosaic manner that if you think that withholding your seed will get you a place in heaven, you should bear in mind that all the eunuchs will be getting there first.

In case you don't know Bhagat Kabir ji, he was a weaver by trade and a Buddha (awake) in his own right. To illustrate his wisdom, I'll say that when two disciples, who apparently wanted detailed intellectual instructions along the mystic path, approached him in his youth, he explained simply:

"Path presupposes distance; if He be near,
no path needed thou at all.
Verily it makes me smile to hear of a fish in water athirst!"

o o o

I placed all the books I had in the back of my hatchback (the book had two distributors but they only ordered a box or two at a time) and I took my leave. I was a vagabond again. I had spent in Seattle six years, practically unnoticed; becoming a non-famous, self-published author and a middle-aged dancer was much more work and rejection than praise.

o o o

At one time I had friends in Port Townsend, but the bartender at the restaurant where they used to work explained that they didn't work there anymore; they had left town. As I

---

‡ *Buddhism: A concise introduction* by H. Smith and P. Novak.

strode out, a song popped up in my mind; it was Carole King singing:

"So far away; doesn't anybody stay in one place anymore?
One more song about movin' along the highway. . .
. . . I sure hope the road don't come to own me. . .
Yet so many dreams I've yet to find . . .
. . . So far away."

o o o

I camped by the Columbia River for a few days, among towering ponderosa pines, the majestic Mount Rainier looming nearby. It was a time to relax, appraise and plan a course of action. Beyond my campfire, the nights were cold but clear. I slept under a blanket of stars, atop my boxes of books, in the cozy little cave they formed beneath the roof of my hatchback.

o o o

It is said that it is always cloudy and gray in Oregon, but in Portland I remember many sunny bright days, shady trees, and downtown streets teeming with people; it must have been springtime, for I hardly ever start traveling during winter when I am up north. In one of such days, a band (maybe it was a big stereo) was playing at Pioneer Square, so I fetched my dance shoes and danced with all the ladies who cared to. And for a magic interlude, while dancing by myself, the music took me away and I became the *dance*.

In downtown Portland, I also found a huge indoor shopping mall, and following the pungent smell of spicy, good food reasonably priced, I found the food court. Lo and behold! I found mango juice in that court, a delicious mango juice that I have yet to find in any other shopping mall in the country.

Also in Portland, during a rainy Friday afternoon, I went to see the young editor of a newspaper called El Hispanic News, with whom I had made an appointment. After perusing the book, he agreed to write a review, and was kind enough to send me a copy while I was still in the San Francisco Bay Area.

o o o

In San Francisco, I remember having lunch with a fellow hosteler in Chinatown—the largest outside of Asia. The place was packed, boisterous, vibrant. In this particular restaurant, the waiters maneuvered and wiggled graciously around the tables, with delicious food on their trays, while the patrons selected what they wanted guided by the spicy smells.

o o o

I always had to arrange and schedule my book signings on the spot, as I arrived, with whoever was willing in the chain stores that carried the book, so my visit prolonged several weeks in the area. Hence, I had to switch lodgings frequently, for hostels only cater to travelers, and only allow a limited number of days per stay. So I got to know all the hostels (and bookstores) in the Bay Area, from Hidden Villa to Saratoga.

One night in which I was denied shelter at the hostel in Sausalito, I had the privilege of traveling in the heaviest downpour I have ever seen. It is not a figure of speech when I tell you that it was coming down in buckets. It was!

It was unbelievable. I remember looking up at the deluge in alarm, wondering. The gutters and some streets had become threatening torrents. Part of the freeway disappeared in the diluvium, and I had to take a detour that got me lost while on my way to San Jose. I stopped at a restaurant to ask for directions, and I couldn't help but to ask just like the song sings:

"Do you know the way to San Jose?"

They looked at me askance, but when convinced that I was indeed lost, they gave me directions. Next day, on the radio, I heard that such diluvial downpours occur every one hundred years or so. No wonder.

o o o

I took my friend Marian across the bay, I had met her at the Fort Mason hostel. She was from France, a ski instructor who didn't mind dancers.

I wanted to show her Telegraph Avenue and the University of California in the famous city of Berkeley—I'll tell you more about Berkeley later. That day we also visited City Lights.[††]

After browsing in a store, Marian would ask concerned, "Did I take too long?" I was impressed.

I remember her bright smile, her slender but voluptuous built, and her deep brown eyes that matched her long, thick hair. We were just new found friends getting acquainted, and when I hugged her goodbye that night (she was leaving early next morning), I figured that the distance would make us forget each other soon, so I didn't jot her address down.

Did I regret that? I didn't realize how much she had affected me until she was gone. Then, a feeling of irreparable loss took possession of me. And when I finished my book signings in San Francisco, I took my leave, taking also with me that profound feeling of loss.

It was inexplicable. It was overwhelming. I remember crying like a child all the way to the following city where I was going to stop at a Waldenbooks to see if they had enough copies of my book in stock. I remember that tears were streaming down my face and I couldn't stop them.

When I got to my destination, I had to use eye drops to hide the signs of my inner turmoil and be able to converse with the manager. And back on the freeway the deluge started again, almost all the way to the city of Monterrey. It had no precedent that experience, and there was no real or immediate reason for it. So I figured it was caused by some sort of travel fatigue; it brought to mind a painting I saw in Seattle.

While in Seattle, I obtained permission to rehearse at the convention center, close to my apartment. And there, I once saw an art show presenting the work of Andrew Keating. This particular piece was titled: *Traveller.*

It struck a cord in me that painting, for it portrayed perfectly well the desolate landscape and emotional turmoil that a wandering nomad will face at times. It is said that when the Buddha started on his journey to awake, he was at times, by his own

---

[††] City Lights is a landmark bookstore and publisher in San Francisco; it was a famous center of protest during the sixties.

admission, terrified when amid the anguished shrieks and frightening roars of the jungle night.

I concluded later that the devastating feeling of loss was not only due to losing Marian's friendship; she was also a catalyst. She stood for all the women who had vanished in the receding road.

I realized that I had to face the fact that I couldn't have both lives: I could either be a homemaker or a wanderer but not both. We all have a road to travel; we have to accept who we are in life's stage. I also saw that I was missing perspective; I was being overwhelmed by the ego and feeling sorry for myself. I was still trapped by the programmed mind.

There is nothing here that stays unchanged from moment to moment, nothing at all; change is permanent. Even for a relationship that lasts, there is always constant change, for better or for worse; it changes from day to day, from year to year, from decade to decade; it dissolves eventually. Sometimes it grows stale and meaningless. Our problem is that we don't see this; we don't see that we should love unconditionally, for whatever length of time it is meant to be, and then, let go.

o o o

I saw their faces, smiling, changing, disappearing in the mist of time, ceasing to exist: memories and thoughts with no substance. Gone.

o o o

It was somewhere around Monterrey, when heavy rains delayed my trip; a bridge collapsed somewhere, and the area became an island, so I was stranded. I do remember that I was by the beach, for the police woke me up at about 2 o'clock in the morning to let me know that the roads were open and I should keep moving—no sleeping or camping allowed on the beach.

I should explain that sometimes the police feels like talking to me due to my way of life. But most of the time they are helpful, and in the type of situation just mentioned, they let me stay overnight. The officer may even give me his name as reference in case another officer comes by. Of all government officials, I believe police officers to be the best at dealing with the public, for they have to deal with all kinds of situations. More than once, I had been well advised by police officers with the best of intentions.

But occasionally, I am out of luck and meet with an asshole, who may even throw me in jail for a couple of days. All I can do in that case is to use the third attribute of the *art of stalking*: forbearance. The officer in such a case is probably a rookie, an absolute beginner.

o o o

I was charged as follows: loaded handgun in the car in public property, allegedly for protection (a couple of guys had tried to rob me a few weeks before). It did not matter that I was behind the house where I lived; I did the landscaping there, and the address was on my license. That access road was not part of the property, they explained. It was a public road.

Thus, I got a glimpse into our justice system: You declare yourself guilty, even if you think you are not, to get less jail time. They scare you with the possibility of being found guilty and spending more time in jail. I tell you, you need to know your ropes to deal with these people, and a good lawyer.

My time in a cell was brief. Yet, walking down the dark long corridor of the county jail to get booked was ominous: rows of cells, endless bars, a feeling of doom, of entrapment. But the officer who booked me made me laugh while taking my mugshot:

"Your five minutes of fame," he said.

Mine may be the only smiling mugshot in the world.

I asked another officer if I could do my three days in a work crew. My offense was a misdemeanor so he didn't mind. They added me to a landscaping crew assigned to a nearby park, with a warning: I was serving time in jail, if I missed one single day, I would be back in for six months. Ugh!

My fellow inmates were decent folks. I thought they were friendlier than most of the people I had met in town. One of them offered me a free tire rotation upon getting out, and gave me the address of the shop where he worked.

They told me about a guy, who had just been released; they thought he would be back, a psycho. But I didn't meet him.

Have you ever wondered about the many people in jail who should be out, or the many out who should be in? Some of the latter might even be sending the former in; jails are a business.

o   o   o

Despite that rude awakening at the beach, or maybe because of it, that night I *dreamed* that I was in a city somewhere in Southern California. I entered a building, which was sort of an outdoor shopping mall, and pleaded with a middle-aged lady who was sitting by herself at a food court, to tell me the town's name.

Apparently the lady didn't talk to strangers or she was in a bad mood; she ignored me completely, so I approached a young couple who was chatting at a nearby table. The man seemed to be annoyed at the interruption, but the woman smiled and obliged me. It was, however, a name that didn't make sense. It sounded like San Luis Obispo but not quite. I remember looking at her and repeating the town's name.

"Chan Jit Obit?"

She nodded. I was puzzled, but not wanting to show that I was an alien in their world, I thanked her and left.

That *dreaming* experience was so vivid, and the people's demeanor so real, that when I stopped in San Luis Obispo, I drove around a while to see if I could find the shopping mall. I couldn't, although the town looked similar. After about an hour or so, I gave up. It had been another world.

Everything is a Mind projection, either individual or collective. Our daily life is more real than an individual *dream* because it has the power of many; we are *dreaming* it together. We build a *dream* in which we enter at birth and exit at death; it is a collective agreement. Birth and Death are part of an agreement in a dream. Whether the *dreamed* place is an actual place in this world or our own creation, the experience is as *real* as our daily world is *real*.

o   o   o

When I arrived in Santa Barbara late one afternoon, do you know what was playing at the movie theater in State Street? *Marian's Wedding.*

"Dammit," I thought.

Nevertheless, the hostel I found was an effective distraction; the rules were few and ignored; television sets blared all night; rudeness was the norm. During my sole night there, I heard a few arguments and the rumblings of a fist fight. It was a rathole.

Santa Barbara, however, is known casually as the American Riviera, due to its Mediterranean climate. It is not only an alluring coastal town, but also a busy tourist destination. So I soon found part-time work in my favorite pizza restaurant, and to save money (rent is high), I slept in my car. I camped, so to speak, on Garden Street, by the Alameda Park, which is located a couple of blocks from State Street; it was allowed.

At the time, the park covered three blocks and one of them was dedicated to the area trees. All the trees had little plaques that told you their origins, their species, how are they most useful to humans and so on. I learned the names and species of most of the trees in that park. There was a tree there named Tipuana Tipu, originally from Africa, highly valued as a shade provider due to its thick foliage.

There is another park in Santa Barbara along Shoreline Drive, with long winding pathways, tall pine trees and manicured lawns. It sits on sheer cliffs over a seemingly endless beach, and it gives you a superb view of the Pacific Ocean. I used to do hatha yoga in that park; I did it early in the mornings, just after going to the gas station, and before taking a shower at the Beach House for a couple of dollars.

o o o

Let me tell you about this book signing I did at the Earthling Bookstore. There wasn't a big crowd at my talk by any means, and only one of the attendees bought a book.

But after my audience left, I stayed and sold a few more copies by handing out flyers. H____, the owner of the bookstore, had been kind enough to help me get an interview in a radio show a few days before, and I wanted to sell as much as I could for her.

The radio interview was odd. I did not know how to pre-pare for it, or even if I should. I just went to the radio station.

Some of my coworkers told me that it went well, but they didn't fool me. I remember while being interviewed, asking my host if she had read my book. I don't think she ever did.

How can you interview someone about a book you haven't read and do a good interview? She responded to my question evasively. I could tell she was groping in the dark, improvis-ing. I also remember an awkward moment of silence after one of her peculiar questions.

o o o

I used to practice dance at the University of California in Santa Barbara. When I finished, I showered in the old gym.

One night, I was just beginning to shower when I turned around to see a young guy looking at me while masturbating. Lo and behold! The last thing I wanted was a confrontation with a weirdo, so I was about to skip my shower that night, when suddenly, in a flash of inspiration, I said emphatically while looking into his eyes:

"You are sick!"

The young man stopped as if I had just slapped him; he looked at me aghast. I had him; the sudden, timely impulse had been effective. I continued:

"You need to see a doctor. You are . . ."

The man vanished. He just disappeared. I do not remem-ber seeing him leave.

o o o

Are we really getting an education in college? Are we disre-garding true knowledge? We don't learn to discipline our minds; we don't learn to see how our ego controls our lives by rendering us blind and obliterating our connection to the Spirit. Our learning has no spirit. We are just getting programmed.

Do you remember *The Wall* by Pink Floyd? "You are just a brick in the wall . . ." True! Through our so called "education" we become the bricks in the walls enclosing our ignorance; we become just another brick in the system's walls.

Our social contract is a sham.

o o o

Before I left, I *gazed* into a stone. On three sides I *saw* animals: canines and birds mostly. The owl I *saw* was about to take flight. On the fourth side, I *saw* a well-dressed man without a head. I interpret the visions to mean that the owl would be my guide on the road, and that from the people I would meet I shouldn't expect much.

The latter was a no-brainer. How can anyone expect much from beings who are in such a sorry state? We don't run this world, the ego does, and the ego is such a blinding little beast. All we can expect from blind beings is the spur that will help us overcome our own blindness.

o o o

Gazing is like meditating. Its purpose is to stop the random chattering of our mind. *Gazing* is one-pointed concentration on an object or place. We *gaze* with eyes partly closed, and when the chatter that prevents our *seeing* stops, we will have the *vision* or the *dream;* we will enter then the realm of the *other.* What you *see* is not a drawing in the stone due to its crevices and shape, it is a *world* that can pull you in if it is strong enough—a window, so to speak.

Some stones will tell you nothing.

o o o

There lived in Shoreline Drive an older lady that was totally absorbed in her inner chatter; so absorbed she was, it wasn't internal for her anymore. She was one of those persons who the world considers to be a little crazy.

She would trudge out of her house, turn around, and talk out loud to some imaginary person in the porch. She repeated that pattern almost all the way to the bus stop, about a block away. When about to reach the bus stop, she would stop addressing the house but continued talking to herself until the bus arrived, and probably beyond.

But you see, that lady was not acting much different from most of us; we are all trapped by thought. We all have an inane internal dialogue. Her's was out loud, that's all. And that is what the ego does to human beings; it traps us in a world that *does not really exist*. But don't take my word for it. Keep a close watch on your mind and see what you find; it is the first step toward *awakening*.

o o o

Upon arriving in Los Angeles, I was lucky to find a work exchange position to secure a bed at the hostel in Santa Monica. This hostel is quite busy due to its location on Second Avenue. It is a block away from the Third Avenue promenade, a popular tourist destination where most shops and restaurants are located. And perhaps due to its convenient location, at the time of my visit the staff was extremely rude to the hostelers on a regular basis—I heard they still are.

Hence, when opportunity knocked, I moved to a work exchange position in the Fullerton hostel at 1700 N. Harbor Boulevard, adjoining the Brea Dam Recreation Center. The old building was formerly a private home, it is now a quaint, little hostel with a relaxed ambience and a cozy fireplace.

o o o

Trees and shrubs were abundant in the semi rural property. And I soon learned that our fierce black cat could dispatch any rodent regardless of its size, age or speed; she was a hunter.

Thus, the hostel was a haven for her, for the area was inhabited by a great number of rabbits, squirrels and many species of birds. And although she had to be aware of my friends the owls and other birds of prey, I think she enjoyed the singing of the mockingbirds.

I was once enjoying the flight of two impressive eagles myself, which were circling the sky above, when suddenly the higher bird folded its wings to a sharp angle and swooped down. Upon reaching its mate, it spread its wings again, breaking its fall, and they both flew away for a change of scene.

The only drawback of living in this hostel was the golf course located next door, which frequently sent the golf balls flying in our direction as projectiles of destruction; the huge safety net was useless. They hit my car twice, breaking my windshield once. Dangerous! The owners paid for the new windshield. But that guy Mike, he was hilarious. He was upset because I had parked *there*.

They were all hilarious in that golf course; the manager told me once that I couldn't hike bypassing their area because it was dangerous. Hell! It was dangerous to sit outdoors in the hostel; they barely missed me a couple of times *there*. But again, what can we expect from such an obtuse and contradictory species.

Take D___D___, for instance, he was the live-in clerk at the hostel, and he was a treat. He was one of the greatest snots I have ever seen; and therefore a lot of fun, many buttons to push, an unabashed itsy-bitsy, teeny-weeny petty tyrant. D___D___ was from the East, but he was the complete and total opposite of Mahatma Gandhi. He was remarkable!

Petty tyrants are always a help in our quest to subdue our own ego, and D___ D___ was my helper to the very last minute. He was both: a challenge and a joy. Did I have to use control, discipline, forbearance and timing? Bless his soul!

Chapter 6

Recapitulation

When my selfless acts cancel my selfish acts my account is closed and I am free of Karma. The Karma of the old acts cannot apply to the new person.
                                                    —Ecknath Easwaran

According to Castaneda, we need a detailed recapitulation of our entire life in order to get rid of the negative energy left in us during our social interactions, and to recover the energy we left behind in those interactions. It is akin to clearing our Karma.

The recapitulation was done by recollecting each event, while turning our head from right to left, inhaling deeply to recover the energy we left behind; and turning our head from left to right while exhaling, expelling any foreign energy left in us. It was to be done within a wooden crate, which would be destroyed at the end. The destruction of the crate symbolized the end of our former life, a rebirth.

While working at the Fullerton Hostel, I built a small enclosure with branches; it was to be my wooden crate. I built it on a hill behind the hostel, hidden among trees and bushes, and only accessible from the road that led to the Brea Dam. The place was higher than the building and practically invisible.

Sometimes, I sat up there in recapitulation, as early as 3 o'clock in the morning, or as late as midnight, amid the crawling noises of fearlessly approaching wildlife. I remember a possum one night, scurrying away at the end of my flashlight's beam, like a dog pulling on a leash.

o o o

I had started working on my recapitulation in Seattle. I had learned about it in Castaneda's *The Eagle's Gift*, while I was in Zipolite. It was by chance that I found the book, lying on a shelf in Gloria's place.

When I started my recapitulation, my *dreaming* was still sporadic. I would find myself in unknown places, sometimes walking along deserted streets.

Visions would come occasionally, when I was still awake but beginning to fall asleep. Sometimes they were pleasant, sometimes grotesque. I would see a woman at times who would try to talk to me. I could see her lips moving, but I couldn't hear a word she said, or read her lips; then she would vanish.

I did not know what to make of these visions. Then Castaneda's *The Art of Dreaming* was published, and I got several more pieces of the puzzle. I understood then that the visions were the first stages in *dreaming*. I also learned that what I had encountered during previous *dreaming* sessions were different kinds of inorganic beings.

As you probably remember, allies disappeared from my life when I put *dreaming* on hold in Barra de Navidad due to my uncertainty. Since now I knew who they were, I figured that the energy recovered doing my recapitulation, would help me to bring them back and communicate with them, and I could go from there.

o o o

I had postponed my life's recapitulation thinking that I needed a wooden crate to do it, but one day, while still living in Seattle, something urged me to start in my walk-in closet. I started with the most important events in my life; then I passed to the sexual relationships, which are supposed to drain the most energy. And later, while in Santa Barbara, I wrote a detailed list of events, so that I could do a thorough recapitulation.

I did find the recapitulation to be a useful in some ways. At times, while recapitulating, I found people so similar in behavior that they were almost one and the same; I could have recapitulated them together, eerie. I would also see traits in people that I hadn't seen when I had been with them.

An important fact that I verified in my recapitulation was an insidious self-importance in all of us; it is equally there in the old and the young, the poor and the rich. I remember recapitulating a conversation with an individual, in which I realized that he was so wrapped in himself, that he didn't really care to hear anything I could have said.

The prevalence of self-importance became thoroughly obvious to me one day that I was working as a parking lot attendant in San Diego. That day, someone complained about a drunkard who was being obnoxious. I found him sprawled on a corner of the open lot.

When I explained to him that he had to leave, he started mumbling unintelligibly, while glaring at me with bloodshot eyes through his filthy, straggling hair. Then he fumbled into his pockets, took out a twenty-dollar bill, and hurled it at me while arrogantly screaming:

"I have money! I have money! Call me a cab! I have money!"

Sometimes, to try to make people aware of our predicament, I propose a simple game: For ten minutes or so we can talk about anything we want, but we can't use the personal or possessive pronouns I, me, my or mine; we can't refer to ourselves in the third person either. As soon as the game starts the conversation slows down greatly; it might even stop, for these pronouns are omnipresent, and to avoid them, we have to think before we speak.

The game helps us realize how much the syntax of our language is centered on our *self*—language is definitely a need and tool of the ego. Most often than not, it might be better not to talk at all. But we are trapped in a world of form, of multiplicity, so we have no choice but to use language to communicate. It is important, however, to *stalk* ourselves; that is, to be aware when we speak that language is a powerful tool with serious drawbacks: it can mislead or distract us; it can edify but also destroy.

o o o

An active recapitulation is something to practice regularly; that is, be here and now without judgments, and don't take offense at anything. If your ego is not involved, if you act self-lessly, you don't give or receive negative energy because nothing is taken personally. That means you have nothing to forgive and nothing to remember, for you were living with presence.

This does not mean that you will become everyone's doormat. Still, if you need to stop someone, do it without anger or hate. Remember that humans are trapped in the ego's net.

o o o

Perhaps my recapitulation did help my *dreaming,* for it was at the hostel in Fullerton, where I unexpectedly started using another *dreaming* technique. Somehow, without *intending* to do it, I would awake from one *dream* into a second *dream,* and then into my *dream* in the daily world; it would just happen.

But, although I found the recapitulation helpful, I also found limitations to it. I will discuss those in due course.

o o o

My mother died suddenly of a heart attack.

I had made contact again while I was still living in Seattle, for the image of a little girl started popping up in my mind. I didn't know why the occurrence, but I figured that maybe somewhere in South America a little girl needed my help. And I discovered that I had a nine-year-old niece, who really didn't need my help but wanted to meet me, and that my mother was also living in South America. I sent them a copy of my book.

After my disappearance some fifteen years before, everyone was happy to hear from me, for they had thought that, perhaps, I was dead. In a way they had been right, that *I* was dead.

o o o

A few months before she died, my mother wrote me a letter asking me to forgive her. So I wrote back to forgive her; I told her that everything was forgiven. Everything *is* forgiven.

Although she should have known, for she was aware that I consider everybody my helper. Everything is interconnected. One way or another, everyone is our helper. Let's forgive! If we must struggle, let's do so without hate or envy.

o o o

I had been toying with the possibility of visiting my relatives, and after my mother died, I couldn't postpone my visit anymore. But publishing and promoting my book were not financially rewarding endeavors, and my part-time job was barely allowing me to pay my debts, so I was wondering how to fly to Ecuador and back.

Since I was sort of a prodigal son who had not returned and wouldn't be returning anywhere, I didn't think that my mother had left me anything. But Carla, my sister, said that she had left me something—not much, but something. So she would help me with my traveling expenses, and I could pay her later.

o o o

My sister did not prepare me. We climbed into her car and she took me to the cemetery. I was expecting the customary grave but only found a tiny compartment where my mother's ashes lay.

o o o

My niece was crazy about me while I was in Ecuador. She had been expecting me with anticipation; I was legend for her. And she wrote for a little while after I left. Then she vanished; eventually, her mother and my brother-in-law did also. I can't complain; I guess they were taking after me.

o o o

My cousin Lydia helped me to get some paper work done so that I could receive my little inheritance. She wrote me a letter saying that she had liked my book a lot. Lydia said that she didn't know why, maybe because I wrote it.

I understand that my cousin John used a Xerox copier to get his copy. He liked it also.

My cousin Cher, the one who used to live in New Jersey, told me in an email that she hasn't read my book. She doesn't care to.

But she said that she can't understand. "So hard," Cher said about my life, "why?" She completely refused to accept my new identity and cut off all communication. Cher also said she looks swell at her age.

When I was a child, my cousin C___ L___ married a native from Peru and moved with him to a remote town in the mountains of that country. Sometimes I wonder if she is still alive and well.

Everything vanishes. Have you noticed?

And I bet you would like me to reveal some of my personal history. But you have to allow me to draw a curtain on my past, right? After all, I was once a follower of Castaneda, and I learned that, when polishing our link to the Spirit, personal history and its concomitant self-importance, are obstacles that can be quite burdensome and must be reduced to a minimum.

o o o

I wrote a letter to Kristy, my new dance partner. We met in a dance class. I was wooing her. She was engaged to somebody, but I didn't think she was in love, just impressed by his status. If only I would have had more time, but she was leaving soon, to be married. I wished her the best; she had a challenge ahead, and we are all so good at self-delusion.

". . . My friends from college they're all married now . . .
. . . Their children hate them for the things they are not
They hate themselves for what they are
And yet they drink, they laugh
Close the wound, hide the scar
But you say it's time we move in together
And raise a family of our own, you and me

99

Well, that's the way I've always heard it should be
You want to marry me, we'll marry
You say we can keep our love alive
Babe, all I know is what I see. "

In the song *That's the Way I've Always Heard it Should Be*, by Carly Simon and Jacob Brackman, she sees the danger ahead, but resigns herself to do what she is "supposed to do."

o o o

"One more time," I said to myself.

The hostel's backyard was located behind the kitchen, along the entrance road that ended at the Brea Dam Park after making a U-turn. It was a concrete yard with a rough, uneven surface that was full of crevices and depressions. It was also the only place where I could rehearse.

One last time meant that I was tired and pushing myself. While doing a pirouette my left foot got stuck somewhere, and my lower leg stood still while my knee pivoted as if it had an axis. A ligament snapped. I felt and heard the snap; it was followed by an overwhelmingly sickening feeling. Then, I went in denial and tried to keep dancing; an excruciating pain shoot up from my knee.

It was Super Bowl day. Why wasn't I watching the game?

I took a shower, wrapped my knee, and went to work delivering pizza. After rush hour, I asked my boss to send me home with an extremely swollen knee. The next two days I was off and I used them to rest; I never missed a day's work.

The knee had also been dislocated, but after about a month or so I was able to mend it. I did it by slowly and deliberately climbing steps while putting all my weight on it, until it popped back in position.

What a relief! It had been popping at every step. Since I didn't care for surgery, and the knee was healing, I canceled the appointment I had at the University of California Medical Center in Los Angeles.

It took me months to heal that knee. Now, after many years, it is the right knee that slows me down a bit when I dance. Odd!

o o o

Incompetent managers had a common excuse for not bothering to set up a book signing: They'd say that my book wouldn't sell in that particular location. I proved that argument wrong so many times. I did it thus:

After a few months, I'd go back to the bookstore. If the new manager was also an obstacle, I would wait a few more months. When I finally booked a signing in that store with a receptive manager, I would sell all the books ordered for the signing.

D___, who was Waldenbooks' manager at Stonewood Mall in Downey and always eager to sell books, told me, when I explained my problem, that he couldn't understand their attitude. For every time I did a book signing, he ended up with a few hundreds more in the cash register, and that was good.

To compensate, I would set up shop on my own at colleges and universities, from where I would occasionally be asked to leave in spite of the book's educational content. The University of California in Los Angeles gave me permission to sell the book on campus, and I took advantage of the permit (I think they'll forgive me) to sell at their Los Angeles Times Festival of Books without paying for a booth; I couldn't afford one.

o o o

It was during the book fair when I shook hands with an individual you probably would have considered a thoroughly despicable character, but I didn't know who he was until after. The smallish man stealthily approached me and extended his hand while greeting me courteously. I guess he needed to confess his crimes to someone, and, since I was promoting my book, he probably figured that I was a good listener. Authors get into interesting conversations precisely for this reason.

It was a hot Sunday afternoon, and to protect myself and my books from the sun's direct rays, I had set my bookstands on a bench, in the shade of tall eucalypti, on a busy pathway.

The man looked right into my eyes, and without flinching he burst forth:

"I was in jail recently; I was a pedophile."

I had no time to recoil in disgust; his words gushed out as if they had a will of their own. He said that when he was born in Mexico City his parents left him in a trash bin. The passerby who found him took him to an orphanage, where the dismal conditions, disgusting food and extremely cruel treatment forced him to make a desperate escape when he was still a child.

"The place was horrifying," he grimaced.

Scavenging to survive, he found a degrading life in abject poverty. He also found the sexual abuse that would gradually turn him into a sexual predator.

The words kept pouring out of him as if he couldn't stop them. He said that he had understood how base he had been. He said that he was undergoing treatment, turning his life around and becoming a good man. Then, the man said:

"I don't hold a grudge against my parents. I know they must have had chains that pushed them to do what they did, just like I had chains that pushed me to do what I did."

He shook my hand again, with no reluctance on my part, and vanished among the strolling pedestrians.

o o o

Regardless of the outcome, my book tour was indeed a worthwhile endeavor. It was an educational experience.

It was also a way to *stalk* myself; the work itself mattered; triumph or defeat was irrelevant. If the expected results did not materialize, so be it? I was not taking anything personally, and petty tyrants were my help and joy, helping me to reduce my self-importance. Since I was already aware of the sorry state of the human psyche; that is, the fog and the venom in self-importance, promoting my book was a way of interrelating with the world, while breaking free from the conditioning of a dysfunctional social contract.

o o o

In his widely read book, *The Four Agreements,* don Miguel Ruiz, also a Toltec shaman, gives us four agreements to help us break free from our limiting belief system and egomania:

1. Don't take anything personally.
2. Don't make assumptions.

3. Be impeccable with your word.

4. Always do your best.

It is noteworthy that when practiced consistently the first three agreements will take us to inner silence. The fourth is to do our best, just our best, while practicing the other three.

"All Paths Arjuna lead to me."—Krishna

Chapter 7

Don't Die Until You Die

Even to maintain your body, Arjuna, you are obliged to act.
—Krishna

Meditation in the midst of action is a billion times superior to meditation in stillness. —Hakuin Ekaku, Japanese Zen Master

A reason for which I was attracted to the teachings of Don Juan was that they include ways of acting from every conceivable position our daily struggles could put us in. Regardless of how mundane or difficult the situation is, there is always a strategic plan of action to be implemented.

We live in a world of action, and in *The Active Side of Infinity*—his last book—Castaneda puts the following advice in his grandmother's words:

"Don't die until you die."

She was addressing her adoptive son, Antoine. And she was advising him to not just stand to look around but to do something, anything he wanted to do, but something. And I quote:

"Be happy and do. Do! There is the trick. Do!"

Indeed, we live in a world of action.

o o o

By coincidence, I found a bookstore in Santa Monica that sold metaphysical books. There I saw for the first time Castaneda's *Magical Passes* (tensegrity) in videotape.

The concept of redistributing energy with movement is not new. Tai Chi's purpose is the channeling of the energy called *ch'i* to turn it into *jing*, which can be directed outwards. In the martial arts what matters is not the physical blow, but the control of the mind required to deliver the energy blow.

Legend has it that it was Bodhidharma, the first Buddhist monk to reach China, who started the martial arts (kung fu), when he found his monks in terrible physical shape and easy prey for bandits. And G.I. Gurdjieff added to his teachings for the harmonious development of man, some *dances* that he had learned in a hidden monastery in Tibet.

But at the bookstore, I also saw announced some workshops that required a fee, and I was taken aback. I could not recall don Juan ever charging Castaneda a penny for his teachings; they were the Spirit's command. His income, as with any true spiritual teacher, came from other sources so that he could remain impartial.

Nevertheless, I had been struggling recently with the constant and useless chatter that clutters our mind, and I decided to try them. I started by memorizing a video.

As Tai Chi does, the magical passes channel our energy. They bring clarity of mind by bringing our attention to the movement itself and silencing our internal dialogue. It is remarkable though, that some of the passes are done sitting or lying down, with hardly any exertion on our part, to achieve results and change our outlook.

In some cases, the effects are startlingly obvious. I remember an early Friday morning in which I was feeling exhausted; it had been a long, hard week in landscaping. I remember doing a few subtle passes while working, and vanquishing my fatigue for the rest of the morning.

o o o

My promotional tour ended in Los Angeles. The road beckoned again with its bends and promises, trying to draw me away from the city's hustle and smog. Was I ready? Have you ever lived in Los Angeles? I closed all my business connections with distributors and bookstores, and placed the book with a print on demand publisher* so that it would stay in print.

I was still thoroughly convinced that Castaneda had left a map to Infinity itself, even if I had my doubts regarding Cleargreen and its motives. Although Castaneda himself may have been exploiting the teachings and succumbing to his greed, I knew that Toltec knowledge had a sound foundation. I wrote a farewell letter to my friends in Canada that expressed my feelings in the matter. Part of it read:

"I must find the last stretch of my road; it promises to be the most interesting part yet."

And I took my leave.

o o o

September of 1999 found me on Interstate 40 (which parallels or overlays Route 66) heading to Arcosanti, Arizona, a small community founded by the famous architect Paolo Soleri. Arcosanti boasts to be the "City of the Future," that is, a city that will grow upward—no urban sprawl. I had found the concept interesting, perhaps a solution to our pollution problems. I was also looking forward to try life in a rural intentional community, with a group of people who, supposedly, shared a common purpose and lived a full, vibrant life close to nature, conserving an ecological balance.

Responding to an email I had sent, they informed me that a full time landscaping position was available. I decided to try them. I planned to live there part of the year, and maybe travel part of the year; it would be my home base. During my first interview with KZ (the landscaping director) she said that my traveling plans agreed with Arcosanti.

o o o

My first months in Arcosanti were fabulous. I loved the place with its rocky desert hills, cliffs, canyons, and impressive lightning storms—talk about roaring thunder. There were

---

* Xlibris' services brought the book to a standstill. Disappointing!

monthly concerts, and sometimes we danced in the auditorium. It was mandatory to complete a workshop of five weeks to become a permanent resident, and that was an educational endeavor. It was also fun!

We helped in Arcosanti's construction; we harvested the olives and worked on the vegetable gardens; we did the landscape; we welded and did woodwork; we worked in the kitchen. During our last week, we chose a field to specialize in: woodworking, welding, landscaping, cooking, or working at the foundry making the famous Soleri bells.

Consequently, I was surprised to hear from a stone that things would turn sour. It happened one day after work. I was out in the desert chaparral practicing the magical passes, when it occurred to me to talk to an interesting stone. I found a shady place behind some bushes, and *gazed* at the stone until my concentration was complete.

The stone communicated! Three sides gave me visions of people engulfed by great anguish. The fourth side had a man lying on the ground, perhaps dead. He had long hair and a long, unkempt beard.

The visions were graphic, but I couldn't believe the stone. It had to be a mistake. Was it lying? Did I misinterpret? Five months later everything had changed.

In a meeting in which I expressed my feelings of dissatisfaction toward a negligent and incompetent administration, I saw the distress, the anguish and the tears. All was revolving around the man with the beard and others like him, who shouldn't have been there in the first place, for they were troubled individuals in need of professional help. And I remembered the stone!

The concept was interesting, but in practice Arcosanti was not delivering on its promise. I personally handed Mr. Soleri a copy of a letter I had sent to management regarding the matter; he never answered. He even avoided me once at the swimming pool, when our paths crossed as he was leaving. Obviously, our vote did not count.

Arcosanti was run by its founding members, and what they said was final. It was to be expected, after thirty years they had turned inflexible and possessive. Egomania was as prevalent in Arcosanti as it was anywhere else.

I did find Arcosanti's architecture different, but that is not enough to build the "City of the Future" and set an example; a building is just that, a building. Where was the spirit of community? Where was the Spirit?

Mr. Soleri and his staff didn't live in Arcosanti; some of them commuted 150 miles every day to their homes in the sprawling city of Phoenix. Did they really cared about developing a city to conquer urban sprawl? Really?

Therefore, after maneuvering around their egos for almost a year, I left. It was the summer's solstice of the year 2000.

o o o

Most of my time in Arcosanti, I admit, was pleasant, in spite of the rattlesnakes, the scorpions, and the housing shortage. Although I lived in camp, where the crickets, the heat, and sometimes the loud workshop participants were unbearable during the summer months, I loved the place and thoroughly enjoyed my landscaping job: fixing trails, pruning trees . . . building Arcosanti.

It was a joy to hike through the Sonoran Desert, reach the waterhole, and dive into the chilled water from the nearby rocks. I remember a day when, while climbing down a hill returning to town, a golden eagle swooped down by me to alight atop a giant cottonwood tree, which had rooted below by the Agua Fria River.

I had done the hiking trip with my friends Kelly and Chris, but they had decided to take a different route to return to town; I had decided to get better acquainted with the main route. And so it happened that on my way back, I stopped in the shade of a huge boulder to quench my thirst, and the eagle did not see me.

At first I thought it was a turkey vulture due to its huge wingspan, but it couldn't have been. Then the bird turned its head, displaying its powerful beak and its piercing stare, the stare of a bird of prey.

o o o

I remember that it snowed one night the winter I was there. And before going to breakfast the next morning, I ambled through camp enjoying the crunch of the new fallen snow under my boots, the crisp cold air, and the snowy desert landscape. I reached the edge of camp to take pleasure in the smooth flow of the river, and then retraced my steps in the gently falling snow to hike uphill toward Arcosanti. There wasn't much landscaping to do that day, other than shoveling snow downtown while snowballing each other.

o o o

Hiking under the full moon with my friend Jennifer was a pleasure, and it strikes me now that we never consider the mountain lions, which were known to roam the area at times. Alas! But I did mention to her the importance of staying present, attentive. Perhaps she will remember and apply, and if mountain lions are roaming nearby then, she will see them in time to escape.

I remember the majestic cottonwood trees, edging the campground along the river, flaunting their snowy seeds; their leaves rustling in the wind, glinting in the sunlight, fluttering like so many butterflies. I also remember the good friends I made there—men and women who were doing their search: Kelly, Chris, John, William, Katherine . . .

Stasia was the chef when I arrived; she was also an experienced dancer. We started to choreograph a dance concert together to perform in the Auditorium. But we were so disappointed at the city of Arcosanti that we lost all interest. We left, all of us.

We are only passing through.

o o o

Rocks are fun to work with. If you pay *attention,* they will certainly tell you where to place them. They helped me to leave the place looking much better than I found it.

I also helped to build a fence around the twenty-five acres to keep the neighbor's cattle out. It was grueling work! We pounded those posts into the hard desert ground with heavy manual post-drivers, freezing in the morning and sweating at noon through the month of January. When the ground was impenetrable we used picks and shovels, and cement to refill the holes and secure the poles.

But I enjoyed it, in mindfulness, taking delight in the cloudless blue sky, the desert cacti, and the rolling rocky hills. I worked with JD (the man with the beard) and Regis Domadi; nobody else wanted to work with them on a steady basis, although JD wasn't a bad guy really. I remember losing my watch one day, and he taking some fifteen minutes of his time to help me find it. I really liked him better than I liked Regis (the dysfunctional egomaniac in charge), although JD may not believe that. But let me tell you a little more about JD.

Although not young or big, he was extremely strong and quite a hard worker, a small Paul Bunyan. He would have been at home with the pioneers of yore. You could tell that he knew what hard work was just by looking at his hands. I remember once pointing out to him some blood on the handle of his pick:

"That's my blood," he said matter of factly.

He was working with an open blister on the palm of his right hand—no gloves. He never wore gloves.

JD was also an activist who stood for what he believed. His picture was on the front cover of one of the main newspapers in the area once, due to a face-off he had with some strip-miners nearby. The picture, in full color, showed him talking firmly to one of the miners; he was trying to make him understand how they were harming the environment. It was a good picture of him as a defender of the earth.

But somehow JD was off, maybe in need of professional help. He was overbearingly offensive to most people. Wherever he went he taunted and provoked. I guess he felt superior. It was Jones, our construction supervisor, who told him during our daily outdoor meeting:

"I don't know why, but you bring out the worst in people."

That day we were all trying, without results, to make JD see his folly.

o o o

I remember the day I met JD. I was collecting rocks on the slope of a rocky hill for a landscaping project, and he climbed down to chat. I think he was attracted by my old straw hat, which was overly patched with duct tape.

"You look like a survivor," he said.

And we chatted for a while.

I can't remember what we talked about, perhaps about surviving. But although he was friendly (He guffawed frequently), I had to end the conversation, for it was becoming erratic, rather nonsensical. I could tell that something was out of kilter but could not tell exactly what; I never could. The ego was to be blamed in great part, that I could tell. But what else? I did not know.

There seemed to be a hidden meaning behind everything he said. I heard later that he had been in Arcosanti before, in the late seventies, and due to his snide remarks somebody hit him on the head with a 2 x 4. It was said that the guy who hit him went to jail, and later jumped bail and fled to Mexico. JD could really upset people.

When I left Arcosanti, JD was already gone. But I knew he didn't like my hat anymore, for I had been openly in favor of his removal. I wish him well anyway.

o o o

In a story I read in a nature magazine, a she-wolf was raising ten cubs and one of them, who was the strongest of the lot, was hurting the others at play. The she-wolf scolded him twice without success; the third time she clasped his head in her jaws and snapped his neck, killing him instantly. She had to, for his unruly behavior was putting the safety of the whole group in jeopardy.

o o o

Have you noticed how easy it is to leave a place sometimes? In this case, since my friends were already gone, moving on was a breeze. Jennifer was still there but she had killed our friendship a few weeks before. I guess I offended her when, while out hiking, our conversation by the campfire drove us so close that I stroked her hair gently, and softly kissed her lips.

She was younger than me, and I guess that mattered to her. How could I?

Jennifer was unforgiving. She was utterly disappointing; she would flirt if we met by chance as long as there wasn't an audience; in public she was cold, unreachable, even rude, displaying a behavior that I had thought to be below her.

On my last day in Arcosanti we ran into each other in the camp's laundry room. She seemed upset about something, slamming doors and rudely throwing things around. Was she trying to tell me something? Should I have talked to her?

We had shared so much: hiking by moonlight, dinning out, dancing, conversing . . . But she had displayed such a rude and disappointing behavior throughout the previous weeks that my opinion of her had suffered a serious setback. I just ignored her, and left.

William, my landscaping partner, asked me where I was going, and I told him that I was going east. Do we ever know where we are really headed?

o o o

The Hopi Reservation in Northern Arizona is divided into three mesas. The village known as Old Oraivi is on the Third Mesa, near Kykotsmovi, in the northeastern part of the state.

Orayvi, as it is known by the native inhabitants, is one of the oldest continuously inhabited settlements within the United States. The Hopis have always lived in this area, and their roots go back in time one hundred generations or so. Their culture is one of the oldest in the continent.

I was headed northeast, toward the Lama Foundation in northern New Mexico, but stopped at the reservation to visit M___ and his wife J___, in Shongopovi, on the second mesa. I had met them in Arcosanti. M___ had taught us how to plant corn in the Hopi tradition, and how to bring rain clouds in by *grabbing* them with *tiger claws* (a claw-like weed), and pulling them over.

o o o

If you look at the Second Mesa in one of those satellite google maps you'll see an unappealing, barren desert landscape.

Instead, I remember a bewitching landscape, an enticing, rustic beauty. It crossed my mind to stay in the area, but my friends said that to work in any reservation you have to be a Native American.

Before I took my leave, however, I secured a couple of bicycle spokes that I needed to work on my crafts. M___ had a box load of them, so he could spare a few.

I was still traveling in my Plymouth Colt, which could go just about anywhere with its easy to fill gas tank. Amazing little blue car!

o o o

At the Lama Foundation, I found that a recent fire had devastated the region, but new growth was beginning to show among the burnt pine trees, and their unspoiled mountain spring still provided excellent drinking water. Wildlife was still abundant, for the area is practically surrounded by the Carson National Forest. In fact, a young black bear had been recently killed in the property by a ranger, for it had been showing unruly and aggressive behavior.

The Lama Foundation is located 8,600 feet high in the lower slopes of the *Sangre de Cristo Mountains,* and the view from the restaurant (one of two buildings that miraculously escaped the fire) is spectacular. The dinning terrace overlooks wide plains, mountain ranges and the impressive Rio Grande River Gorge; it is higher than the clouds hovering over the valley. Thus, while dinning, you could also be enjoying the approach of a lightning storm from the distant south, while farther north the sun would still be shinning on the land.

The new buildings, although in progress at the time, were already awe-inspiring, massive constructions of adobe and wood. These straw-clay residential buildings were being built with thick adobe walls, which enclosed bales of hay, to provide superior insulation during the harsh winters.

o o o

As a guest, I worked at the Lama Foundation for a few days, but I didn't stay. As a resident, I would have had to pay while also working six hours a day, and I guess that after my Arcosanti experience, the offer wasn't inviting enough; or perhaps I wasn't ready yet for another *community* experience.

I drove south through Taos and Santa Fe, where I stopped briefly to sell my crafts.

Chapter 8

The Sycamore Ranch

*Your own practice can show you the truth. Your own experience is
all that counts.* —H. Gunaratana

I admit that the main reason to go to Truth or Consequences in
New Mexico was curiosity. I had heard, or read somewhere,
that the town had a mystical quality about it.
But Truth or Consequences is a town visited also for its
mineral hot springs. Originally called Hot Springs, it took the
name of a popular radio program in the year 1950, when Truth
or Consequences' host announced that he would do the program from the first town that renamed itself after the show.[*]

o o o

The hostel was a cozy little enclave, as I had heard in Taos,
with hot springs edging the Rio Grande. The attendant explained
that I would probably be by myself in the tee pee, which was
convenient. But if company prone to snoring or farting arrived, I
thought, or if it rained copiously, I could always move to my car.

---

[*]Truth or Consequences' host, Ralph Edwards, came to town during the
first weekend of May for the next fifty years. This event was called The
Fiesta, and included a beauty contest, a parade, and a stage show. The
town is commonly known within New Mexico as T or C.—Wikipedia

Besides two common dorms and the Tee Pee in the back, the hostel had several rooms and a kitchen. By the entrance, there was an office and a few parking stalls. To the right, across a grassy yard and opposite the office, a huge bald eagle stared fiercely at you, as you came in, from the wall facing the stalls and the street beyond.

o o o

It was summertime, late in the afternoon.

Drenched in sweat, I headed to the river and the hot springs as soon as I arrived. And under the ramada covering the tubs, I found reclining chairs where I could relax while enjoying the view: A rock formation that resembled a giant turtle resting atop the otherwise barren hills.

The Rio Grande was flowing gently that day, murmuring softly as it passed by, inviting me to jump in. So I did.

It was exhilarating to dip into the ice-cold water after soaking in the hot tubs. I was planning to stay in the area just a few days. I ended staying for a year and a half.

o o o

Truth or Consequences does not seem like much of a town, to tell you the truth, and it is right in the middle of the Chihuahuan Desert, which somehow raises the cost of living. It is an expensive oasis. So it may seem strange that I stayed that long.

But it happened that Tasim, a hostel employee, was teaching a Yoga class in a building that also belonged to the hostel owners. This building was suitable and available for dancing, and it turned out that a few people wanted to take dance lessons. Therefore, I decided to stay a little longer.

Nothing came of it; after a few classes the building was closed down for repairs. But Truth or Consequences, I was beginning to discover, was an interesting town in many ways; it had unsuspected treasures. I found a hidden dance hall, with an ample wooden floor, where at times musicians gathered for a jam session.

Although the old, scruffy building was usually closed and seemed abandoned, it was not. The owner, a doctor who was also a musician, meant to keep it rolling.

o o o

It was a Sunday, during the Fourth of July festivities, when a group of drummers came to play. It was early evening when I started to dance upon the ignored dance floor of an almost empty locale. It gradually became a spiritual experience in which, at times, the frenzied rhythm of the drummers would take me away. I left late that night, leaving a room teeming with people.

o o o

Through a friend I met at the dance, I got introduced to drumming. Lila and her friends taught me the basics at a medieval festival we attended in northern New Mexico. And she was kind enough to give me one of her many djembes.

A djembe is a drum that has a bowl shape to the top of it and a thin bottom, and is played with the hands. It is a versatile drum; you can get a low bass sound by hitting the center, a medium tone by hitting towards the rim, and a high sound by slapping the rim. I had always been interested in drumming but never had tried it due to my left arm.

I must confess now that as a child I lost some muscle in my left arm due perhaps to a polio attack. It is not apparent in regular social interactions, and it never has hold me back. I served two years in the army, and for a while I was a sharpshooter in an infantry division; nobody noticed. In fact, I was almost sent to Viet Nam (I didn't know better, so I was ready to go), but the time frame in which I served prevented it.

Some movements, however, I can't do well. One reason for which I like to dance is that I can make my own choreography, my own moves. When I tried boxing in my youth, my jab was difficult to control after the second round; playing basketball, I broke it once. So I had *assumed* that drumming wasn't for me.

But I started getting really good rhythms, and having lots of fun with it. Maybe I'll still get to be a master drummer someday. Isn't it amazing how we limit ourselves at times? Until we try, we don't know.

By the way, have you heard about Nick Vujicic? The Australian guy who was born without arms and legs? Nick swims like a fish, surfs in the ocean, and lives a full happy life. Amazing young man! Nick confesses that sometimes he hopes for a miracle to happen, but he is a miracle himself.

o o o

Since there was action in town, I decided to rent an apartment and get a job. Thus far, I had been staying either at the hostel or at the campgrounds nearby. I had been working in the hostel in lieu of rent, and selling my crafts to the guests and to stores. When Tasim ushered me to Gray Street, on the outskirts of town, and showed me Stillpoint, I felt extremely lucky.

Stillpoint was a place oriented toward meditation and the arts, with cottages for rent and two meditation rooms. The place was owned by Mr. S____, an excellent reiki[†] practitioner and teacher. Shortly after I moved in, I got a job at one of the pizza parlors as a delivery driver.

o o o

I moved into my new home with Shirley; she also wanted to stay in town and needed a roommate temporarily. Shirley and I had attended a few Yoga classes together and we liked each other, so I moved in with expectations. She played the flute like an Angel and meditated every morning. Shirley even told me herself that she was "the sweetest person."

Yet, something was amiss. She seemed to be totally wrapped in herself, lethargic. She hardly ate. If I cooked or brought food she would decline to eat or merely nibble at something. Shirley never cooked. She was taking one of my classes one day, and in the middle of the warm up she suddenly left, without a word.

And once, when I pointed out to her that she had jammed my answering machine (right in front of me), due to impatient and careless handling, she proceeded to demolish my expectations conclusively. Shirley underwent a transformation, flying into a rage that showed remarkable hostility and a vicious temper; I thought she was about to hit me. Out of control, she

---

[†] Reiki is a healing technique based on the principle that the therapist can channel energy into the patient, to activate the natural healing processes.

stormed out of the house, slamming the door shut, and yelling that she would move out on Monday—it was Friday night.

Such unwarranted behavior showed that in spite of her meditations, in spite of being a "mature" woman, she was not quite what I wanted in a roommate, or in anything else for that matter. Her behavior marred her beauty.

So I wrote her a note the next day (she wouldn't talk), telling her that she didn't have to rush—I knew that she was close to bankruptcy and looking for work. But, since we obviously weren't compatible, at the end of the month we should go our separate ways. In the meantime, we would be civil and considerate roommates. She agreed; it was the only sensible course of action we could think of.

o o o

We had rented that cottage for a month and a half, hoping to keep it longer if a previous bidder didn't show up. And during our stay, I thought at times that perhaps we could at least become friends; but she was always in dreamland, in a distant past, with distant friends, or maybe waiting for a phone call.

If I mentioned the importance of staying present she nodded; she even mentioned once that a friend had pointed that out to her, but she promptly went back to dreamland. I asked her out once, to the park, to chat, to get acquainted. Shirley agreed. I met her outside, where she was talking to our neighbors; she had changed her mind.

I remember one pleasant evening when we were talking outside, sitting by our front door. For a moment, I thought we were making a connection, when suddenly my phone rang for her—she always made sure her friends paid for the many long distance calls. A few minutes later she returned with an incomprehensible idea in tow.

A friend, who was going on vacation for two weeks, had called from Canada. Shirley was seriously considering to drive all the way up to Canada to house-sit and save rent money, ignoring two facts: It would have taken approximately two weeks to drive that far north, and her rent was already paid.

When with my help she came to her senses, she became despondent; our connection disappeared as if it never had been there. She seemed to have been transported somewhere else, as if she had taken off with her friend.

○ ○ ○

I was lying on my bed one afternoon and Shirley came into my room.

"Can I lie with you?" she asked nonchalantly.

I was dumbfounded. I did not want to develop a relationship with her anymore. But I was polite.

"Sure!"

And there I was, lying beside this lush woman, who I really liked and found physically desirable, but the connection was missing. Her behavior was too erratic to trust, too cold and impersonal for love.

"If I touch her," I thought, "I'm doomed. She doesn't really care."

Should I have held her in my arms? Should I have given her a good fuck? Maybe. But I wasn't good at flings anymore, and the relationship was never there. So instead, I touched her hand lightly and said:

"I gotta get to work." And I left.

Was I punishing her? She never apologized for the aforementioned temper tantrum, and I didn't think she deserved a single inch of me. Her spirituality was merely a mask.

○ ○ ○

It was a cool, balmy morning with clear blue skies.

I saw Shirley ambling along the river bank past my new place. I called to say hello. I showed her my new pad. We visited. I was wondering how she was, but as usual she was distant. She cut the visit short and said good-bye. And I knew then, with certainty, that she had never really cared.

A few weeks later, I heard from our former landlord that Shirley had left town. She was now living close to Denver, Colorado, where she had friends. Shirley had also found work that she liked, and she was well.

○ ○ ○

My new residence in Riverside Drive stood across the street from the Rio Grande. It was a pleasant studio apartment with a back door, and many windows through which the sunlight streamed in, but it turned out to be only a stopover, for I found the Sycamore Ranch.

o   o   o

It was December. I had been rehearsing downtown in the parks and tennis courts. A former student informed me about a loft that I could try.

The loft turned out to be too cold to dance, but while trying it out, the young woman who was in charge told me about a cottage for rent in a nearby ranch. Terri said the ranch was owned by Jean, a sweet old lady who lived with her daughter Donna, and they needed help. I jumped at the opportunity and that very day I made an appointment to visit the ranch.

o   o   o

The Sycamore Ranch is not located in the desert; it rests on a wide canyon, bordered by a forest of stately sycamore and cottonwood trees. Las Animas Creek runs through it, and, according to a plaque I saw in the house, the biggest sycamore (of the species) in the United States lives in the ranch.

The day I went to see the Sycamore Ranch, I took a stroll to what later became my favorite place in the property; they called it the sacred grove: A circle of imposing sycamores located to the east of the house. I sat on a rustic wooden bench to commune with them, to enjoy their company.

Sun rays filtered in shafts through the canopy, warming the cool grove. White-winged Doves cooed in the distance, and the earthy smells of rotting leaves and dry grass merged in the air. A leaf fell on my black felt hat and stayed put. I took it as a good omen. I kept the leaf. On January the tenth of 2001, I moved in.

o   o   o

It is said that the Sycamore Ranch is located within an energy vortex, and due to the extensive *dreaming* I experienced there, I believe it is true. Besides, in my cottage, in the dark of night, I would frequently see inexplicable flashes of bright light.

o o o

The influence of that energy vortex, I am sure, affected the cat. In truth there were three cats, and I don't know why it didn't affect the others. But let me tell you, this particular cat turned into something else.

The evening I met Darwin he introduced himself by leaving a long, painful gash on my right hand. And so I learned that you could pet Darwin but only *briefly*, and playing or teasing was out of the question. In brief, he was not a pet anymore, if he ever was.

We did become friends eventually. But he was a grumpy, belligerent old cat, that was still the terror of the neighborhood; just seeing him coming would send his brethren bucketing into the house, as if they had seen the devil himself. For a good reason though, Darwin could pick a fight to the death with anything that showed signs of life.

At dusk he usually vanished into the forest, toward the creek, to wherever he went to stalk his prey, a cream tabby that blended into the tall, dry grass, a camouflaged cat.

One day Darwin disappeared. I don't know if he ever returned. He was a slower cat in his old age, and maybe one of the owls claimed him; he was no match for the birds.

Or it could have been a rattlesnake. Maybe he attacked a rattler; he was quite capable of doing such a thing, and he had an excuse. For he probably sensed that his end was approaching, and I strongly suspect that he wouldn't have liked being petted even on his deathbed.

o o o

Animas Creek dries about half a mile after it passes the Sycamore Ranch. Only once, after the winter rains, I saw it as a raging torrent reach Caballo Lake. But apparently, in days of yore that creek was a mighty river, for the water table is high in the area, and the Sycamore and Cottonwood trees have grown to an impressive size.

The aforementioned tree, the biggest Sycamore I have ever seen, grows close to the creek, and it is over two hundred and fifty years old. It takes five people, circling the tree with out-stretched arms, to hug its trunk.

o o o

If you enter the ranch, coming from the paved county road, which connects to highway 187 about four miles away, you'll come across a cactus garden. You will see then that the main house and two small cottages, are nestled among huge syca-mores behind the cactus garden; this garden is circled by the dirt road on which you are walking.

If you look to the left of the house, you'll see the vegetable garden. It has a young tree in the middle.

But if you follow the dirt road, which also forks towards the back bypassing the house, you'll enter the forest and find the creek. After crossing the shallow creek, upon the wooden board that is placed for that purpose, you'll find another property farther down, where the road ends. Then the hills (erosion has turned the canyon walls into rolling hills) climb high, turning into a desert plateau.

If you retrace your steps though, and hike up the steep hills located across the road, facing the house, you will get a superb view of the area from the mesa. To the west, the canyon dis-appears among the mountains, which are blue in the distance. Toward the east, it follows the creek for about two miles. Then, Animas Creek continues on its own toward the lake.

Below, to the right of the house, you'll see a barn, and a trail that goes past the barn through an open, grassy field to end at the sacred grove, where three huge sycamores and a few lesser trees form a circle. You will not be able to see the fire pit in the middle, but it is there, surrounded by rustic benches made of old boards placed over hefty tree stumps.

Occasionally, winter casts a snowy landscape, and during the twilight you will see the house below, glowing amid the giant sycamores with the light that escapes through its doors and windows. In the deepening twilight, that house, you can tell, is only a vision in a dream, and you are spellbound.

o o o

When it happened, I was in the sacred grove, sitting on a bench amid the sycamores, *gazing* east. The twilight was giving way to the night, and I almost missed it. But I stood up to stretch and turned around, and there it was!

The foliage in the sycamores surrounding the house was a dark shadow; and behind, the sky was scarlet, an aurora borealis in red. The whole firmament was scarlet. The sight stunned me for a few moments. Then, as I ambled toward the house, it disappeared, to never return.

Two lines from an Emily Dickinson's poem came to my mind:

> "That it will never come again
> is what makes life so sweet."

o o o

The fenced complex was really a hidden oasis in the middle of town: A circle of hot springs in small cloisters, shaded by trees, and sustaining the studio and the house where the owners lived. It became the place were I taught next. I can't remember how I found it.

But I clearly remember the night I met Nicole in that studio, at a dance concert in which we both performed. Nicole was a superb belly dancer. She was also a remarkable woman.

Just because I was new in town, she invited me to her house and took me to see Elephant Butte Lake.‡ She would call me if anything was going on, so that I wouldn't miss out. Not that she was interested in me, for she had a boyfriend somewhere; this was just who Nicole was.

We were planning to do a dance piece together to perform in her next show, so she was taking my class to improve her technique and skills. We thought it would help the piece to be more varied and interesting. Nicole had a group of students, and she brought them to class also, making it a bigger class.

---

‡Created in 1916 by a dam across the Rio Grande. It is the largest and most popular lake in New Mexico.—Wikipedia.

One Tuesday afternoon, after class, she hugged me good-bye. She was going to see her boyfriend; she planned to be back in two weeks.

Nicole left Thursday afternoon, and we all lost her. . . . an accident on the freeway. She was thrown off her vehicle. The ambulance rushed her to the hospital to no avail. On Friday, during the hours before dawn, I lost my best friend in Truth or Consequences.

o o o

The funeral services were held at the park, as she would have wanted. I remember that everyone wanted a turn at the microphone to justly praise Nicole. I recalled a day in which she found me at an event in that very park, an event to which she had invited me to herself.

"___ you came!" she exclaimed, saying my name as if my presence was important, and the warmth in her voice was such as to render me her friend forever. Nicole *knew* that everything is interconnected.

Since I hadn't been her friend for long, I wasn't planning to speak at the funeral at all; but after most of her friends had spoken, I got up on impulse, grabbed the microphone, and said:

"I didn't know Nicole for as long as most of you, but throughout that time, she was a *friend*."

And I sat down.

o o o

Nothing was the same after Nicole died.

"No man is an island, entire of itself; every man is a part of the main. . . . Any man's death diminishes me, because I am involved in mankind; and therefore never send to know for whom the bell tolls; it tolls for thee."—John Donne

o o o

During March, two months after I moved to the ranch, I gave notice at the restaurant. The petty tyrants had done their job, helping me to practice control, discipline, forbearance and timing. I could have quit that job on my first day.

Still, most of my crew mates had been friendly; we had no incidents at our Christmas party in spite of our gang members. I had worked in the place for about six months, long enough to get to know the town and save a few dollars. I had also started working part-time at the ranch, pruning the fruit trees.

We had trees along the dirt road, also in the field located between the cactus garden and the county road, and behind the house—peach, apple, and pear trees. I nursed and pruned the budding trees, thinned their clustering buds, and watered them regularly. We were expecting a good harvest that year.

But the buds were snatched away by an unforgiving wind, as if on purpose, methodically. It blew with a vengeance that year, obliterating our harvesting expectations. Donna told me that when the harvest was good, the fruits were easily sold "right from the porch."

o o o

On a visit to the city of Las Cruces, looking for a challenging jazz class, I found instead a school that needed a teacher. They auditioned me, and I got hired to teach a beginning jazz class.

While I was still working at the pizza parlor, I came across an impressive piece of music that J___ and N___, two fellow workers, were listening to at the end of the night shift while we were doing the dishes. The piece was intense, and I decided that sometime I had to choreograph and dance it.

Thus, when I started teaching in Las Cruces, I talked to the artistic director about my plan. Cindy listened to the music and fell in love with it. We decided to start working on the project. The theme would be the predicament of humankind: The fact that we live trapped by ego, and the effort we must make to break free. The chosen piece of music was titled *Call of the Ktulu* from Metallica SM, that is, Metallica with the San Francisco Symphony Orchestra—classical rock sir!

But it never happened. Cindy didn't really have time to rehearse. And after my summer session, which was extended, classes started closing or diminishing in size for reasons unknown. Even former Miss New Mexico canceled her class.

Meanwhile, the school put a young lady in my class who nobody else wanted, and who should not have been allowed in class at all. She suffered from anorexia nervosa, and I had to send her home due to her seriously faint condition; she could have been hurt. I did not try to renew my contract.

o o o

While these events were taking place, I was also trying in earnest to finish my recapitulation. It was then that I came across the damaging report about Castaneda and his cohorts through the Internet. Since I had verified much of what Castaneda had revealed, and much of it is ancient knowledge, his fact twisting and metaphoric inventions didn't unduly disappoint me. He was only a messenger.

Therefore, I took his deceiving and promiscuous behavior with equanimity; I took it as a challenge. After all, what else can a warrior do?

Nobody here gets out alive.

127

Chapter 9

Mud Shadows

What is the force that binds us to selfish deeds, O Krishna? What power moves us, even against our will, as if forcing us?   —Arjuna

It is a constant challenge for human beings not to struggle in compulsive thinking and just enjoy life to the fullest. And it is astonishing that, although all of us have unlimited potential, we don't seem to care to explore it; we rather indulge in petty fights with our immediate neighbors, and wage war with distant countries. It poses some interesting questions.

Again, in the Mahabharata, when the words of the Bhagavad Gita are about to be given to him, the warrior Arjuna asks Krishna:

"What power binds us to selfish deeds? What power moves us, *even against our will,* as if forcing us?"

When I read the passage, I thought that maybe Arjuna didn't get an accurate answer. Perhaps Krishna, considering his inner turmoil, didn't want to rattle him further—the Hindu Scriptures do refer to outside forces frequently. He answered the question with the words:

"It is selfish desire and anger, arising from the guna of rajas (passions); these are the appetites and evils that threatens a person in this life."

Yes, but why?

"What power moves us, *even against our will,* as if forcing us?"

This question points to the possibility of an alien force. Is there an alien being out there who puts a foreign installation in our heads? Satan?

Castaneda wrote about a kind of inorganic being (mud shadows or flyers) who feed on our negative energy. These beings, to ensure their food supply, supposedly place an installation in our minds when we are young. This installation thinks for us, fostering our narrow-minded self-reflection. It creates the energy the mud shadows like, the outbursts of our ego: anger, envy and hate.

Being aware of humanity's tendency to self-reflect and wantonly destroy, I can understand where the idea of an alien influence comes from. After all, shouldn't we be doing better than we are? Why do our actions contradict our intelligence so consistently? Why our insistent self-reflection? What power moves us . . .?

I found an interesting parallel in the works of G.I. Gurdjieff; when noticing the inability of human beings to confront the fact that we are transitory, he explained the aberration in a similar way: The Powers That Be to keep us blind and prevent us from despairing behavior upon realizing that we are condemned to die, implanted in us the Organ Kundabuffer. It was placed at the base of our spine when we still had a tail.

Gurdjieff was being facetious, I presume, but the fact is that quite frequently we behave as if controlled by little green men from outer space. We are the only species on the planet that is always at odds with each other, with practically all other species, and with the planet itself. We are the only species with wars, jails, ghettos and mental institutions, where we act and live worse than animals would anywhere.

While working in Berkeley, selling my work in Telegraph Avenue by the University of California, I was exposed to the strangest cases of human behavior and mental illnesses. In those days Berkeley was called Berserkeley. Mental institutions had been closed down for lack of government funding, and apparently all the inmates had been sent to Berkeley.

Indeed, some Telegraph Avenue's habitués were in great need of assistance. There was a man, who I frequently saw collecting money for the free clinic; for greeting him once, he cussed me and even mentioned my mother. There was another deranged being, who, to get the newspaper, would kick the stand until it broke; and yet another, who, as he passed by, would yell at you to shut up if you were speaking. Berserkeley!

I also remember in Berkeley, an insane young man who would come to the street with a beer in his hand. There were three or four blocks of vendor stands, and he would start at one end; he would dawdle behind the stands on both sidewalks, bleating like a goat. That man, to me, was representing humanity, bleating in despair through the fog of our own making. How did we arrive at such quandary? What have we done to ourselves as a species? What is the force that binds us to selfish deeds?

Having been in contact with inorganic beings (some of them hostile), and having read in the Hindu Scriptures about the devas, and how we are assaulted "even in our dreams," I was seriously thinking for a while that Castaneda was right. Noticing how our egomania seems to annul our intelligence rendering our species violent and destructive, I was seriously considering the possibility that an alien force could be the cause. After all, the energy brought forth by our divisiveness could be palatable to some sort of inorganic being.

But I have never seen a Flyer. I have seen the other inorganic beings, but never a mud shadow. And once, when Castaneda was facing a gigantic mud shadow, terrified to the bones, although the encounter was supervised by don Juan, he received the following advice:

Don't be frightened, don Juan said imperiously. Keep your inner silence and it will move away.

And I understood then that the Flyer was the ego, which is always defeated by inner silence.

So always remember that when you succumb to worry, fear, anger, self-pity, random thinking or any other unbalanced state of mind, the flyers's mind, the ego-mind, is in control; the Flyer has you by the throat. But don't be frightened, revert to inner silence and it will go away. And if you practice consistently you will *see* that we are all part of the Whole, everything is interconnected, nothing stands on its own, and there is nothing to fear.

o o o

Berkeley was also a haven for extraordinary people. I re-member an attractive young lady without arms, her hands sprouted at her shoulders. And a man, with a terribly disfig-ured face, who wouldn't cover his deformity, like the phantom of the opera would, but faced the world with it.

I nodded at him once, a gesture of acceptance, and he came up to me, so that I could appreciate his disfigurement better. He stood in front of me and waited for a moment, as if trying to impress upon me the notion that, when you were as repul-sive as he was, nobody wants to deal with you, as if trying to tell me that I shouldn't nod at him if I couldn't talk to him.

And the fact was that I didn't know what to say; perhaps today, I would have known; perhaps today, I would have asked him his name. Or maybe I would have told him that we all have a challenge, and everything is interconnected. Perhaps not. But that sunny morning, I merely looked briefly into his brown eyes, the only part of his face that looked hu-man, and he left, without saying a word.

o o o

Don Miguel Ruiz, in his work *The Four Agreements Com-panion Book,* also talks about inorganic beings who feed on our fear and divisiveness, explaining it as mythology and alle-gory: Our own demons (fear, envy . . .) that can turn into allies (love, kindness . . .) depending on our energy and attitude. Don Miguel says that the Judge in us (ego), the Victim in us (also ego) grows to the point of becoming a Parasite that de-stroys our awareness and enslaves us. He explains that our Belief System (collective ego) reinforces the delusive program of our individual egos and magnifies the challenge.

In Castaneda's words: The protective guardian (ego) be-comes a jealous, despotic guard who robs our energy to feed itself, while obliterating our connection to the Spirit.

o o o

The Buddha dispelled my doubts further when he explained: "There is no effect without its cause, and no supernatural beings that interrupt the basic causal processes of the world."

Since the Buddha also says that the ego is not indigenous to human beings, it seems that the *foreign installation* is formed, as Ramana Maharshi says, when the *I thought* sprouts at an early age. Whereupon the ego assumes separation and limitations, and we start creating our troubles. It seems that Satan, the Beast, Mara, the Flyer and the Ego are one and the same.

o o o

Castaneda's *foreign installation* (the flyers's mind) is, like Satan, a psychological spur. The idea that we may be prey for an inorganic being, just as chickens are prey for us, should galvanize us into action. It also cuts us down to size, doesn't it? It turns us from the dominant species into just a remarkable species among many other remarkable species. Castaneda was a trickster.

Nevertheless, it is irrelevant whether there is an inorganic predator fostering our self-importance or not. For the fact is that as a species, we live in a state of constant and selfish preoccupation, which is causing great harm not only to ourselves but to all sentient beings. And it behooves us to control our pernicious ego and discipline our minds, so that we can evolve into human beings with inner sight.

o o o

J. Krishnamurti daresay that being present should require no effort because it is just a matter of being *here*. Why should that require any effort? He also said that we put too much importance on the methods we use to awake: meditation, chanting, mantras . . . because methods imply time, and awakening is in the here and now. And I quote:

"When you see the necessity of it (a still mind), then there is no inquiry into the method at all. Then you see the necessity of having a quiet mind, and you have a quiet mind."

Paradoxically, although awakening is in the present moment, there is an effort to be made, for there is a habit to break: our internal dialogue. And we do need, as the Buddha teaches, the right effort. Presence is acquired with the right effort, for the ego will try to assert itself repeatedly; it will try until we *see* the necessity of a still mind with our very core.

o o o

Shamans instill in their apprentices the habit of breaking routines, because it changes their perspective and forces them to still the mind. When we act from habit we don't need to focus our attention, and our mind indulges in its usual internal babble. So we break routines to disentangle ourselves from the programmed mind, and to help ourselves break free from the habit of compulsive thinking, our most detrimental routine.

o o o

I remember walking at leisure up to Geisel Library at the University of California in San Diego one night (it is a long walk even when you pay for parking), when I noticed my absent minded condition. I had been wrapped in thought, pondering, absent, oblivious to my surroundings. Does it happen to you? Exactly! We are all ponderers. And we miss Reality.

So I decided to focus on what was taking place at the moment. I became aware of the things that I was approaching—benches, buses, cars, bus stops . . . I noticed the aroma of the eucalyptus trees as I strolled along the wooded trails.

Soon I arrived at the last stretch of my walk; the wide walkway lined by towering eucalypti, which takes you directly to the library. I noticed other pedestrians immersed, like I had been, in self-reflection, oblivious to the world.

I noticed the library in the distance, a huge building that rose like a mushroom, like a giant bird spreading its wings and obliterating the star-raddled sky. I pondered how such an enormous building could remain aloft with such a narrow base, a feat of engineering. It reminded me briefly of the ship Nostromo, in the movie *Alien*, and for a moment my mind drifted in that direction. I brought it back.

I continued focusing on my surroundings, aware of the approaching building and the steps that brought it near. Gradually I was awaken from the slumber of self-reflection.

When I arrived at the Geisel Library I was fully present, and the feeling of lightness was such that I felt like prolonging my walk. A quote from the Christ interrupted my concentration again, "Let thine eye be single and your whole body will be full of light."

And then I realized that prolonging my walk really didn't matter, for, regardless of where we are or what we are doing, presence of mind is always an option. Our attention can always be placed on the action at hand.

It does not matter how well we do it either; our best is enough. Do not judge yourself, just be aware of what the mind does—that is the key. To see how we worry about past events that can't be changed, or future ones that will never happen, is the first step.

Stalk yourself! Watch the mind's moves! Make it play! And don't force the issue, for the mind's very nature is to think. If you must think, however, do so about what is pertinent, or occurring now.

Our best effort is advised, for an undisciplined mind can't avoid misleading us. Having a disciplined mind is the only way to control our ego-induced self-reflection, the darkness of selfishness. A disciplined mind is the key to happiness. "Let thine eye be single . . ."

When the Buddha finished his three months retreat, during the season of the southwest monsoon, he would tell his monks that if anyone asked what he did during his retreat, to tell them that he was mindful of his breathing, his body, his mind, his emotions, his feelings, and finally, he was mindful of the phenomena around him.

o   o   o

The act of following our breath will immediately place us in the present moment, away from the morass of mental imagery. Basui and Ramana Maharshi also recommend the method of self-inquiry to arrive at inner silence.

"Who am I?" We must ask the question repeatedly, with the *intention* of bypassing the ego to find out who we really are. Who is reading this? Who wants to know?

o   o   o

At times, when I am about to succeed at stilling my mind, a different dialogue pops up. This time the dialogue is about explaining to somebody what I am doing and how, so that they can do it also. This dissertation seems worthy but it's also useless; there is no one there for me to explain anything. No matter how worthy the dissertation seems, it is empty talk; I am talking to myself, and probably the situation will never happen.

And even if it did, it is not happening at the moment. It's the ego again, the monster with three thousand heads. Zen Buddhist monks say that even thinking about the Buddha is a waste of time. Our sages do not want us to think about them or worship them; they want us to be like them: present! The right thought is the thought reflecting what is occurring right *now!*

Another thing worth considering is that upon gaining ground, a stream of negative thoughts can erupt in your mind. As if *someone,* who knows your weaknesses, is feeling threatened by your progress and trying to stall you. Sometimes the thoughts are incongruous or grotesque, and seem to pop out of nowhere; they are completely unrelated to the present moment. This intruding states of mind, should help you realize that the ego is not only a *foreign installation*, but a *foreign installation,* who, although our own creation, has a will and an energy of its own. And it tries to reassert itself.

The challenge is clearly cut out for us: The ego has to be taken for what it is, a mere point of reference in a dream. Our senses feed us incomplete and therefore misleading information. As don Juan told Carlitos: "*Doing* makes you separate the pebble from the larger boulder. If you want to learn *not-doing* let's say that you have to join them."

We have to bypass our mind.

o o o

Life is full of paradoxes, isn't it? The ego doesn't really exist, it's just a thought. But we need it to be able to operate in a world that is itself a thought, an interpretation of energy, a *dream.* The Toltecs call themselves warriors because the conquest of the self is the greatest of all conquests; it requires a sustained effort; it requires *unbending intent.*

The following quotes go to the gist of the matter. The first one illustrates the challenge that we face; the second shows the way to meet that challenge:

"Lack of vigilance is like a thief, who slinks behind when mindfulness abates. And all the merit we have gathered in, he steals, and down we go to lower realms."
— Shantideva in *The Way of the Bodhisattva*

"The more I doubted, the more I meditated, the more I practiced. *Whenever doubt arose I practiced right at that point.** Wisdom arose. Things began to change. It's hard to describe the change that took place. The mind changed until there was no more doubt. I don't know how it changed. If I were to try telling someone, they probably wouldn't understand."
— Ajahn Chah in *Food for the Heart*

---

* Italics are mine

Chapter 10

My Advisor is Death

Well, let's say that I know all kinds of things because I don't have a personal history, and because I don't feel more important than anything else, and because death is sitting with me right here.
—Don Juan, *Journey to Ixtlan*

Awareness of death is the very bedrock of the path. Until you have developed this awareness, all other practices are obstructed.
—The Dalai Lama

My daily chores at the ranch are done, and, as I amble toward the tool shed, I catch myself immersed in nonsensical self-reflection. I stop the babble, put the tools in the shed and walk out. I cover our firewood with a tarp and sit on a tree stump, in the shade of a giant Sycamore. Sun rays slant downhill into the canyon, promising a hot day. A mockingbird is singing. I inhale deeply the sweet smell of grass.

An ant is carrying something somewhere. She is going far but she knows exactly where she is going. I stand up and follow her until she reaches an anthill where she deposits her load. She moves around greeting other ants, and either she or another ant (Who knows?) picks the load again and enters its underground city.

I return to the stump and notice the grapevines beside my cottage, opposite the tool shed. Some of the grapes are ripe, and I figure that I better harvest some before the deers and the birds dispatch them. I do so, and take some to my landladies.

Then I pondered all I would have missed if I wouldn't have stopped my useless self-reflection. What was I worrying about? Who knows? But it was either past, future or imaginary. The real meaning of the word freedom is liberation from compulsive thinking.

"If you did nothing during the whole of your hour but bring your heart back and place it again in Our Lord's presence, though it went away every time you brought it back, your hour would be very well employed."—St Francis de Sales

Self-reflection not only makes us absent, it also makes us prey for our death, for we forfeit the present moment, when death is always a possibility.

o o o

Using death as an advisor, as an usher to the present moment, is an old technique.

The sage Yudhisthira* is asked:

"Of all things in life, what is the most amazing?"

Yudhisthira answers:

"That a man, seeing others die all around him, never thinks that he will die."

o o o

An accident that occurred while I was still living in Seattle, helped me see that the smallest of our decisions are made in the presence of death; it made the fact perfectly clear. I was leaving my apartment on my way to work, and as I locked the door there was a moment of hesitation. Had I left the stove on? I decided that I hadn't, and I left.

It was one of those rainy, wintry days Seattle is famous for. My apartment was located on First Hill, on the corner of Eighth Avenue and Spring Street. All the parking spaces in that area were metered, so I always parked by the cathedral, some eight blocks away.

---

*The Mahabharata

Buffeted by wind and a light rain, I turned left at the cathedral, hastening along the lee of the building to where my car was parked. And just as I scurried into my car and was about to insert the key into the ignition, I heard a dreadful thud, a massive object had struck the sidewalk. I couldn't see what it was due to the hedge growing along the outer half of the sidewalk, so spurred by great curiosity, I got off my car and ran over.

Lo and behold! A huge cornice had been apparently dislodged by the wind and rain, and it wrecked the sidewalk just where I had been standing a few seconds before. I stood aghast. The distance from the fallen cornice to my car was about the same as the distance from my door to the kitchen and back. The decision not to check my stove had probably saved my life. Death had missed me by a few seconds.

Death as an advisor! We can't feel important when consorting with our death. No matter who we are or what we have, death can, *and will*, cancel it all with a flick of her wrist. That is certain; only when it will happen is uncertain. We must make our plans for the future while ready to die today.

o   o   o

Have you noticed that I consider death a female? I guess that that was what don Juan meant when he told Castaneda that the way we see our death is personal. I see my death as a female figure in a black, hooded cloak. She is rather cold, pale and impersonal but shapely and somehow appealing. I guess seeing her this way dulls the edge of my fright, and if I always use her as an advisor, I presume soon there will be no fear at all. Who knows, she may even guide me through the eye of the dragon.

To keep death as an advisor, as a witness to everything we do, also requires effort in a sustained manner. Not only we have our own ego to contend with (the ego is a liar and the father of them) but our collective ego (social contract) is an impressive obstacle. The socialization process has been efficient at making us feel safe and eternal. It is an ongoing challenge, isn't it? Everyday it starts anew.

o   o   o

I was in the park one afternoon, cleaning the interior of my car, while two birds cavorted in the sky in their daily rituals. Suddenly, I heard a bang right next to me; one of the birds had hit the cars's windowpane, apparently flying at full speed, and he was now lying on the ground. I picked him up tenderly, but it was useless; he lay on my hand writhing in convulsions, dying. His skull was broken and bleeding. I ended his misery.

Next morning, this was in the news: Two men were walking near a construction site downtown, and a falling iron beam swung down on its tether to kill one of them instantly. The other man was in shock but otherwise unhurt. Death is always at arm's length, to our left. Isn't it amazing that we are still alive?

o o o

Late last evening, I took a stroll to the grove of sycamores. And again I caught myself thinking rubbish, worrying about future events—my future at the ranch is uncertain. I stopped. I brought death into the picture, and death brought the present into the picture.

It is cloudy. Birds are chirping aloft. I can hear the cooing of turtledoves in the distance. A light rain starts to fall through the shafts of light cast by the setting sun, but the trees protect me. I am amongst friends.

Within the sacred grove, it starts to get dark, but around the surrounding terrain there is still light. I can smell the rain.

As darkness descends, the birds stop chirping. The forest to my left starts filling with the noises germane to the approaching night. Insects start buzzing; something is crawling through the thick undergrowth. Owls are hooting atop their high perches, chatting with each other. I hoot and they hoot back.

The place is magical indeed, and it agrees with my death, the future doesn't exist. All we have is the present moment, a fleeting instant, so fleeting that nothing really exists.

The Buddhist sage Nagarjuna said that things are so impermanent that there is no way to point at something and call it impermanent. The minute you single it out, it has become something else. All is energy in motion; there aren't things in a flow; there is only flow. Birth and Death are always here, now. As you read these lines there are hundreds of people dying, and hundreds of people being born. All of them, are us.

Birth and death thus, do not exist; they are only part of a flow, of an *interpretation,* of an *agreement.* They are just items in a *bubble of perception*, in the *illusion* of consciousness, in the *dream* of life. Magic! What we perceive as the world is magic; we are magicians.

Nagarjuna also said that there is no difference at all between nirvana and samsara. They are not mutually exclusive. The world of form is a projection of Mind, and part of It. In Castaneda's lingo, the *dreamed dreams* the *dreamer.* Thus, I dare say, the Tonal is a projection of the Nagual, of the Unborn, the Uncreated; they are not a true pair. And this is a *dream* that we can change, an *agreement* that we can modify.

I strolled back to my cottage with the certainty that I have to *stalk* myself continually, especially in the morning. The moment before totally waking is a vulnerable time for me. I am easy prey for self-reflection then, for to regain its hold on me, the ego will unleash many a vengeful ghost from the past. That means that as soon as I am conscious, I must bring my attention to my breathing and my surroundings, to the moment, to who *I* am.

o   o   o

One night, I went to the sacred grove taking a ladder and a rope with me; I meant to visit with my friends. For safety, I threw one end of the rope over the largest tree, and tethered the ladder to a branch on the opposite side. It was a long ladder that barely took me to the first branches of the tree.

As I came near the branches, I found a sizable protuberance close to the main branch, a *chair*, so to speak, where I could sit. About a foot higher, the main branch forked out to stretch parallel to the ground; it forked again before meeting the neighboring tree, and one branch shoot up straight through our neighbor's branches, while the other headed down and south toward the road and the hills.

Some of these branches (to give you an idea of the size of these trees) are as big as grown trees themselves; sitting astride one of them, you feel as if you are riding a horse. On the main branch, I placed a blanket; the *chair* felt slippery with the blanket, and it was too high to take chances.

While sitting astride the branch, the trunk of the tree was my backrest; sitting on the *chair*, the branch was my backrest. I spent about four hours *gazing* into the moonlit night, altering my awareness, communing with the trees.

To relieve aching muscles, I alternated between the *chair* and the branch. I would have stayed all night, enjoying the August full moon, but the threat of rain was in the air; thick, black clouds were rolling in, and there was thunder and lightning in them.

But I returned.

o   o   o

Of all the trees, that one was the closest to me; it presented me once with a quartz crystal rock. It happened that one afternoon, when I was sitting by its roots, I had the urge to get some crystals to help me in *dreaming,* and I voiced my wish. A couple of days later, I found the quartz crystal rock within the hollow of the main root, right next to where I had been sitting. It could have been there all along, I know, but I sure hadn't seen it before, and I *gazed* there frequently.

Donna told me once, that the tree growing amid the vegetable garden had appeared to her out of nowhere. It was just lying there, in front of the house, roots and all, soon after she wished for it.

o   o   o

During autumn the sycamores shed their leaves, and their foliage turns orange and yellowish-red, with a touch of gold and a hint of fire in the glowing colors. From the benches in the sacred grove, I can see the canopy above, as a blend of greens and reddish-yellows. To the west, a few clouds are tinged orange underneath, and to the east, our neighbor's sycamores are gleaming yellow against the fading blue of the darkening sky; it is the twilight during a warm November evening.

The energy vortex must have helped me that night, for I had the longest *dream* I have ever had. I awoke at about two o'clock in the morning and couldn't get back to sleep. My time to leave the ranch was approaching; Donna and Jean couldn't hire me any longer, and I had decisions to make.

But I managed to relax. I grabbed one of my quartz crystals, pressed it between the index and middle fingers of my left hand, and closing my eyes I shut off my internal dialogue. I looked for the color orange. Different shapes appeared, shadows which moved and pulsed. I focused on them. I was facing the sacred grove, and I silently asked the distant trees to pull me toward them.

The next thing I knew, I was looking at a few stone buildings: a house and lesser constructions. I did not try to go through the vision but to hold it as long as I could.

I was not able to visit the trees that night, I have to admit, but after that vision, I found myself inside a strange enclosure from where I couldn't leave or even look outside; it had no doors, windows or roof. It was dark, obviously the darkness of the night, but I could not see any stars.

I *intended* to fly out but somehow I couldn't. That was unusual, but I was reluctant to waste my *dreaming* energy trying to fly; I decided to go through the wall instead, something I had never tried before. I moved forward and went through the brick structure. It was a strange sensation, like going through jelly. I felt myself inside the wall for a moment, and then, I *intended* myself through it.

Outside, I found myself in an unknown city of strange appearance. I have a vague memory of structures and buildings with dome roofs, ending in slim needles as dark as the sky itself; they were unfamiliar and unrecognizable.

There have been times, when I had been unable to recollect a *dream* due to its outlandish contents. Only a fleeting memory remained, a memory of something that just didn't make sense, for it was out of my normal range of perception.

I can't remember how I changed the *dream*. But after I left I was able to fly, and I reached an altogether different region. It appeared to be a South American city in the mountains. I was moving close to the ground, trying to figure out my whereabouts. I started to look for signs that would perhaps give me a hint, but I couldn't see any. I landed on a high, narrow sidewalk, and entered an unpretentious hotel with a cozy outdoor patio by the front desk.

There were no signs of any kind. It was probably a phantom city, but it didn't cross my mind to intend *seeing* any of the few persons who were walking about oblivious to my presence.

But after I came out of the hotel, the dream changed again, and a *pigeon* landed close to me, behind a board attached to a chain-link fence. I could only see its tail, and it couldn't see me. But it started to slowly climb down, so I figured that upon clearing the board and seeing me, it would take off flying. The *pigeon*, however, kept climbing down after looking right into my eyes.

It occurred to me then that it wasn't just a *pigeon*, whereupon I looked fixedly at the bird intending to *see* its energy. The *pigeon* turned then into a blob of energy; it became a circle with bright long filaments all around, and a blackish, churning energy inside. It didn't seem dangerous or threatening but it looked grotesque; I decided not to communicate or try to follow it to its realm.

If it would have been as endearing as the blue scout, maybe I would have followed it; then again, maybe not, Castaneda's Blue Scout turned out to be a hoax. The being whom he had supposedly rescued from the inorganic being's world turned out to be P___ D___ born in Pasadena, California.

Besides, following an inorganic being to a world you don't understand, where your energy can be trapped indefinitely, did not seem to be an intelligent risk to take for any reason. Since trying to figure out what is fact and what is fiction in Castaneda's work is quite a challenge, and considering that allies were of no help to him in vanquishing his self-importance, I guess I made the right decision.

o o o

A young woman was going through the front porch of the main house to knock at the door. As I glided toward her to greet her, I started to feel dizzy. She hadn't seen me, and I didn't want to yell and startle her, but the closer I got, the dizzier I got. I fought the fainting spell and woke up.

I then closed my eyes and saw a huge house cat. He was almost as big as a full-grown German shepherd. As the cat came near, I could see that he had unusually large weird ears, like a rabbit. Allies can take the most outlandish shapes.

o o o

I found a heading, on the cover of a science magazine, which I thought interesting. It seems that scientists are getting closer to the truth, at last.

It read:

"You are a hologram."

And I just read, in a recent issue of *Discover* magazine, that scientists are having to formulate a new theory to explain gravity, because the last theory does not support the latest findings, for instance: *non-location.* My suggestion to them is to delve into the Heart Sutra.

"Form is emptiness. Emptiness is form."

The Buddha *saw* all this.

Chapter 11

The Fire Within

According to the Dzogchen teachings of the Nyingmapa school of Tibetan Buddhism, advanced practitioners can end their lives causing their bodies to be reabsorbed back into the light essence that created them; a manner of passing that is called the "rainbow body."   —*Graceful Exits,* S. Blackman

You are not the body; what difference does it make if it disappears in one way or another? There is no great merit in such phenomena. The loss of "I" is the main fact and not the loss of body. Identity of the "Self" with the body is the real bondage.
                                              —Sri Ramana Maharshi

As you undoubtedly remember, it was at the Sycamore Ranch where I came across the documents discrediting Castaneda's work. By then, I had begun to wonder how long the recapitulation would take me, for no matter how diligently I worked, the recapitulated episodes would always surface again. The only way to effectively keep them past was focusing on the present. Moreover, my past seemed boundless, there was always more to find.

Thus, I began to suspect that the more you give your attention to the past the more it entraps you. Eventually, Sri Ramana Maharshi confirmed my suspicion when he said that the attempt to recall the past is a waste of time; the load from the past forms the present misery. I also found that, according to the Yoga sutras of Patanjali,* the impressions of past thoughts can't be totally removed until we vanquish the ego.

In addition, the recapitulation did not work for Castaneda. The recollection of your life is supposed to be offered to the Eagle (Infinity) in lieu of your life force, so that at the moment of death you can burn with the *fire from within,* taking "nothing you didn't bring and everything you brought." Castaneda tried to hide the causes and circumstances of his approaching death, so that his followers could claim that he had burned with the *fire from within,* but he had not.

Bear in mind also that taking "nothing you didn't bring and everything you brought" implies a *you* somewhere; it implies that the ego is real and can survive after death, but don Juan himself said that, "the idea of a *self* had no value." The ego is only a point of reference in a bubble of perception; it becomes an obstacle; it is going nowhere. As parts of the Whole, we have always been *here!* Where can we go?

Therefore, I decided to look in other directions to take new bearings. I decided that my guru was, at the very least, unreliable.

Since I had put much work into the recapitulation, I decided to finish it in clusters and send it off. It's gone, my offering to the Eagle.

o   o   o

As previously said, however, the recapitulation did help me in some ways; it gave me new insights. It also helped me to understand how similar and repetitious all of us are due to the entrapments of the ego. Sometimes, while recapitulating, I was appalled at the realization that I could repeat a senseless pattern of behavior forever. I still could if I am not careful, if I don't *stalk* myself, so enslaved are we by our social contract and the repetitive mind.

o   o   o

In Buddhist lore, to be *awake* is to perceive Reality as it is *now*; to perceive without letting your beliefs or ideas inter-

---

* Patanjali was a yogi sage considered to be the incarnation of the deity Adi Sesha

fere, without conceptualizing or evaluating. Awakening happens in pure perception; *awake* means *present*.

Your attention will get you to wisdom. Past and future, like the ego itself, have no substance; they will vanish in your presence. In presence, this is a *dream*.

We don't really exist. Although, we do. Don't try to reason this. Be still . . .

o o o

In presence, we will also know how to proceed; we will be directed to what we have to do. It could be something trivial, like washing our dishes, but it is something that has to be done.

It is when we indulge in our internal dialogue, when we let our minds wander, that we waste time, create mischief, wreak havoc and lose merit. In the Buddha's words, those who meditate do what they should do and don't do what they shouldn't do. Our aim then, is to bring our attention *here,* and stay present when we engage in action.

The Buddha's Dharma is very much contained in the following verse; it goes to the gist of the matter:

"Reality as it is becomes the right view for the meditator.
Thinking of it as it is becomes the right thought.
Awareness of it as it is becomes the right awareness.
Concentration of it as it is becomes the right concentration.
Action and speech become aligned then to reality as it is.
Then the meditator develops and is fulfilled."

o o o

Maharshi explains regarding *the fire from within:*

"The gross body is only the concrete form of the subtle stuff—the mind. When the mind melts away and blazes forth as light, the body is consumed in the process. Nandanar is another whose body disappeared in blazing light."

"In the Golden court he shined as Camphor-flame and merged with Lord Shiva."—Nandhanar Shevashrama Trust

148

o o o

Although Castaneda himself was not impeccable enough to burn with *the fire from within* during his exit from earth, he succeeded in making us aware of our possibilities. In India, since time immemorial, Yogis have been able to walk on fire, levitate, disappear in thin air, and lie unscathed on sharp glass or nails.

In the book *Graceful Exits—How Great Beings Die* compiled and edited by Sushila Blackman, I came across ways of dying in which the Self left the body in full awareness, through the *gate* at the top of the head, which remained hot. Sometimes there would be traces of blood in the nostrils or the mouth indicating the passing of the *Self.*

But I also came across three instances in which the gurus' bodies disappeared. In a recent case (1952) only the fingernails and hair remained. In the other two cases only flowers remained. One of the latter was Kabir, the great sixteenth century lay saint whose large following included Hindus and Muslims.

It is said that after his departure, his disciples were quarreling over who would keep his remains, and over the manner of conducting the funeral ceremonies. Above the din, a voice was heard instructing them to remove the burial shroud. When the disciples lifted the shroud, they found nothing but a beautiful array of flowers. The Muslims, who still revere his shrine, obediently buried half of them in Maghar. The other half was cremated with Hindu ceremonies in Banaras.

o o o

According to the yogi Paramahansa Yogananda, the founder of the Self-Realization Institute in California and author of *Autobiography of a Yogi*, a human being who has developed his connection with the Spirit can dematerialize himself or herself at will. He says: "Though scientists now understand that matter is nothing but congealed energy, illumined masters have passed victorious from theory to practice in the field of matter control."

In *Autobiography of a Yogi*, Yogananda points out that science nowadays is proving, what yogis discovered long ago through the practice of Yoga. The equation $E = mc^2$ what really means is that matter and energy are one and the same. In other words: Matter per se doesn't really exist; we *intend* it.

Max Planck, father of the quantum theory and Nobel Prize winner says, "There is no matter as such! All matter originates and exists only by virtue of a force (what Toltecs call *Intent*). We must assume behind this force the existence of a conscious and intelligent Mind. This Mind is the matrix of all matter."

Sri Yogananda explains that with the electron microscope, it was discovered that the electron has the characteristics of both: a particle and a wave, meaning that it is both: matter and energy. And I quote: "Light velocity is a mathematical standard or constant not because there is an absolute value in 186,300 miles a second, but because no material body, whose mass increases with its velocity, can ever attain the velocity of light."

This brings us to the law of miracles. According to Yogananda, masters who are able to materialize and dematerialize, or to move with the velocity of light, or to use sheer energy to bring into instant visibility a physical manifestation, have fulfilled this lawful condition: Their mass is infinite. Or we could also say that they are one with *It* (no ego interfering) and therefore, there is no time or space for them.

o o o

In his book, *Buddhism is not What you Think,* Steve Hagen talks about an experiment in quantum physics, in which an electron sends a photon traveling in wave form at the speed of light into the universe. The receiving electron, in a distant planet, absorbs the photon and vibrates in response sending a return photon.

Apparently, many experiments have proved that the responder's return signal is received by the sender, at the same moment the sender first sends out its signal. The transaction is simultaneous from any two locations. To the photon *there* and *here* are indistinguishable, which means that the universe doesn't seem to have any size or duration.

o o o

Castaneda's Death Defier has a counterpart in India: Babaji. Yogananda writes about having met with Babaji, a being who has been alive for centuries and materializes at will. He hasn't died; his connection with the *Essence* is such that he exits and enters our *dream* at will. Babaji has promised not to leave until the end of this period in history to help his lineage, of which Yogananda was a member.

Paramahansa Yogananda entered *mahasamadi* (a yogi's final conscious exit from the body) in Los Angeles, California on March 3, 1952, after he gave a speech at a banquet. He left us a message in his passing: "He looked on March 27 as fresh and as unravaged by decay as he had looked on the night of his parting, On March 27 there was no reason to say that his body had suffered any visible physical disintegration at all."

It has been documented that the body of St. Theresa of Avila and other mystics, have not shown signs of decay in centuries. We must consider therefore, (to paraphrase Yogananda again) that perhaps not all the laws of the universe are stated in the textbooks of modern science.

In the Gospel of Thomas, the Christ says: "When you come to know yourselves, then you will become known, and you will realize that it is you who are the Sons of the living Father."

o o o

Psychic powers, however, may be more hindrance than help, for they tend to feed our ego. The Sufis[†] regard miracles as obstacles intervening between the soul and God. And some masters of Hindu spirituality urge their followers, to pay no attention to the siddhis (as they are called in India), which may come to them as a byproduct of one-pointed contemplation. They warn that developing psychic powers can distract our soul from Reality, and set up innumerable obstacles on the way to awakening.

It is said that the Buddha while giving instruction to his disciples on one occasion saw one of them practicing levitation. He pointed to the levitating disciple and said:

---

† Sufi, a Muslim ascetic and mystic.

"This, will not conduce to the conversion of the unconverted, nor to the advantage of the converted."

And on another occasion:

"By this you shall know that a man is not my disciple: that he tries to work a miracle. It is because I perceive danger in the practice of mystic wonders that I strongly discourage it."

o o o

Two disciples of the Buddha were resting by the bank of a river, and one of them bragged:

"Look what I can do!" He then pointed his finger at the opposite bank and wrote his legible name.

"Oh, that's nothing," said the other. "I eat only when I am hungry, and sleep only when I need to."

o o o

In the dark, brisk winter night, Las Animas Creek slithered among the rocks, whispering its farewell as I roamed the property. In the distance, a dog barked at the starry sky. I thanked the place for having given me shelter, and as I wandered among the trees I wished them well; I said good-bye.

That night, the rising waning moon kept me up late in the sacred grove. I remembered a summer night in which I had to relocate a rattlesnake. Two foolish cats were harassing it in front of the house, by the grove of sycamores. Darwin knew better; he was keeping his distance. The rattler was rattled and rattling, so I chased away the cats to calm it, and fetched the hand net. Then I scooped it up and headed toward the forest.

Along the way, the snake struck twice; my intentions were unknown. It couldn't reach me though. I thought to drop it across the creek, but, have you ever crossed a stream in the dark of night, tottering upon slippery rocks, with an angry poisonous snake in tow? Precisely! So I deposited my bundle by the creek's bank, and returned on the morrow for the net.

That night, however, the rattlesnakes were quiet, sleeping. When temperatures begin to warm in April, the snakes come out of hibernation.

o o o

Rattlesnakes play fair; they warn you.

I was climbing up a steep trail one day when suddenly I heard the rattle—it has a metallic quality to it, like electricity passing through a wire. Then I saw the viper, coiled and ready to strike. The rattler spoke again: "Stay away," it rattled, "or I'll bite you." I sidled around at a safe distance, and trudged away without further ado.

o   o   o

Early next morning, Pepper and Holly, the new puppies, disappeared with my sandals while I packed; they probably ate them—fewer items to pack. After I finished loading all my possessions into my car, I hug my landladies good-bye. They wished me luck.

On September 11, according to the media, some planes had been hijacked, and two of them had been flown into the main two towers of the World Trade Center in New York City; another had been aimed at the pentagon. Around 3,000 people had been killed that day. I was going to face a changed world.

At the moment, however, the towers weren't a concern, for I was heading toward another ranch in northern New Mexico. Some friends, who practiced the Toltec philosophy under the tutelage of don Miguel Ruiz, had invited me over. I had met them through the Internet, and I was looking forward to communicate with people who had similar interests.

o   o   o

It was the month of February of the year 2002. But winter had been particularly mild that year, so when I arrived at the property, there was but little snow on the ground, although the ranch lies in the foothills of the *Sangre de Cristo Mountains*.

It must have taken me a couple of days to reach that ranch, but the directions Kristy sent me were accurate. The county road, which I easily found, led me practically right to their house, which was located close to a small pond. And I was told by my hosts that during winter you could usually skate in that pond.

Next morning, Kristy and Dan guided me on a short hike to the initial slopes of the mountains; and after a brief but spunky climb onto the foothills, there lay before us the stunning view of a magnificent but deserted valley; the harsh winters have driven away most of its former inhabitants. Cattle grazed in the distance, flanked by continuous ponderosa pine forests.

The property has several houses, a barn, a huge corral and many apple trees; some sections (it is huge) are rented for pasture. A spring is born nearby, and part of it flows through makeshift irrigation ditches, to water some of the apple trees that prosper by the main house.

Dan and Kristy also had the two friendliest dogs I have ever met and some skittish ugly cats. They also had two horses, and one of my assigned chores would be to help Kristy clip their hoofs. I also would have the privilege of pruning a wise, old apple tree (the biggest I have ever seen) and we became friends.

o o o

The purpose of my visit had been to get better acquainted, and perhaps stay through the summer when a Toltec festival was to be held in the ranch. But, after conversing with them, I got the impression that Kristy had joined her Toltec group mainly for socializing purposes; Dan was hardly interested in it at all.

Besides, to get ready for the festival, they needed specialized help, which I couldn't give—plumbers, electricians, carpenters. So I decided to leave. And to avoid the possibility of being trapped by snow if the weather turned, I only stayed a few days.

But it happened before I left, that in the quarters assigned to me on the ranch (a smaller house close to the grand apple tree), I saw, for the first time, a book titled *The Tibetan Book of the Dead,* the translation by Evans-Wentz. Since I had always been curious about the book, I picked it up at bedtime. I opened it at random and read something like this: After we die we'll see some pleasant beckoning beings of dull light that we should avoid; they will only create suffering. We must head toward the intense, blinding blue light.

At the moment, however, that was enough reading for me. I had worked that day enduring cold weather and a harsh, unrelenting wind, and I was exhausted. I thought about the world of the inorganic beings; a world, according to Castaneda, we have to go through when we leave this world in order to gain our freedom. I remembered also reading in the introduction to the Bhagavad Gita about the parallel world of the devas. Then I fell asleep.

Months later, studying more in depth *The Tibetan Book of the Dead,* I saw some parallels between the Bardo[‡] and the sulfurous world of the inorganic beings, which Castaneda describes at length. I read that what we'll find, whether it is heaven or hell (if we are hindered by the ego and don't reach the intense blue light) is of our own karmic making, a karmic illusion we create. And after, according to them, we are doomed to return to the world of form.

o o o

I will leave soon. I am sitting down on the floor while stretching in second position. My chin is on my left knee, while I grab my left foot with my hands. Negative thoughts emerge: Is humanity condemned to egotism? Is the effort to free ourselves futile? Suddenly, I feel a presence and sprang up to an erect sitting position; I realize that the ego is at work. I *see* the enemy within, the parasite that relishes my feelings of helplessness. I brush it off. I am *awake.*

And I remember a Zen Buddhist story in which a man is being chased by a tiger and he gets to a precipice. In despair he grabs a vine and starts a precarious descent to escape, but there is another tiger at the bottom. He looks up and sees the ravenous tiger and two mice, one black (night) and one white (day), gnawing at the vine. He looks around and sees some strawberries growing on a ledge. He plucks one, eats it, and thinks:

"How sweet it is!"

Let's enjoy the strawberries.

[‡]The Bardo is the world in between reincarnations according to Hindu scriptures.

Chapter 12

Seeing Energy

Man can no longer afford to look at what exists outside himself as nothing more than form—in most cases lifeless form. He must begin to see the reality around him in terms of energy.
—Behaving as if God in all life mattered, M. S. Wright

New Orleans is one of the oldest cities in America; it has a multicultural heritage, a unique ambience, a distinctive flair; even on the street corners of New Orleans you can hear music that will stop you on your tracks. The city is the birthplace of Jazz. And in a small park, close to the river, stands an immense oak tree, which is presumed to be around 300 years old, if it survived hurricane Katrina.

For New Orleans also has the power and the threat of the mighty Mississippi River, which runs through it, and can be a devastating force during a hurricane. The city is practically surrounded by swamps and besieged by mosquitoes, for it was built below sea level, but I guess this is part of what makes it unique. I like New Orleans; I like its French Quarter with its ornate balconies and cobbled streets, but I can never manage to stay in the city more than a few weeks.

o o o

It occurred that when I left New Mexico, I stopped in the city of Austin, Texas to work a while. The city is known in some circles as the Music Capital of the World, so I figured that maybe I should explore it.

I found work in the shoe department at Macy's (then Foley's), while I tried to land a dance teaching position. I almost did.

I was a substitute teacher for a night, and my students were raving about my warm up; they told me later that they had felt its effects throughout the week. But after my trial class, the director said that my warm up was inefficient. Inexplicable! Perhaps old age, the last enemy of a man of knowledge, was advising me of its approach with subtle signs and rejections.

Other than that I was doing rather well in Austin. After landing that sales job, I rented a one bedroom apartment in a gated community, where I also secured a place to practice. To top it all, Foley's had a magnificent array of itsy-bitsy, teeny-weeny petty tyrants with whom I could practice control, discipline, forbearance and timing. From a warrior's perspective, it was a great arrangement.

Although it seemed incredible that with such dysfunctional management the store was doing well. Imagine what they could have accomplished with good leadership. Imagine what they could have attained with managers, who would have understood that a worthy leader doesn't oppress and dominates, but serves and motivates. Alas! The possibilities! The possibilities!

o o o

Austin is also known as The Allergy Capital of the World by the locals due to Ragweed and Cedar; from October to April I endured continuous allergy attacks. And this fact became the perfect excuse to leave. The truth was that after being rejected as a teacher by all the dance schools within distance, I didn't need an excuse. I needed a change to rejuvenate myself.

The road was beckoning again. I know now that it will eventually take me to my final destination; I have an appointment somewhere.

Now far ahead the road has gone,
and I must follow if I can.
Pursuing it with eager feet,
until it joins some larger way
where many paths and errands meet.
And wither then? I cannot say.
— *The Hobbit,* J R R Tolkien

o o o

I had started buying and selling imports and novelties to make some extra money, so I decided to risk my savings and put an online store. And because traffic to my store would take a while to develop, I decided to move to New Orleans with the idea of entering the market located in the world famous French Quarter—New Orleans' cultural hub. That would be, I thought, an interesting and profitable venture.

But the market rejected my stuff because similar merchandise was already being sold on site; they also preferred crafts. Maybe I should have tried with my own work, but I had put that aside for the moment due to a lack of business, and, to tell you the truth, it didn't even cross my mind.

Fate? I missed hurricane Katrina.

Instead of going back to Texas, however, I decided to continue toward Tampa Bay in Florida. I was drawn to the area by an intentional community, which was supposedly developing near that city. After my Arcosanti experience, I was wondering if there was any substance to any of these so called, "Intentional Communities." Besides, I had been told that the flea markets in Florida were huge, and everything sold in Florida's Tampa Bay.

o o o

But before I take you to Florida, let me tell you about this nightclub, and a few other interesting places that I visited before I left New Orleans; after all, New Orleans is an interesting city. The nightclub was not in Bourbon Street—the licentious street in the French Quarter best known by tourists. It was not in the French Quarter at all.

I can't remember the club's name. Everybody at the hostel that night was going to Bourbon Street. But I wanted to see this nightspot that had been recommended to me, as a place with excellent music where the locals gathered. So I went by myself, and I found this fine group of performers playing dynamic rhythms that were meant to be danced.

Do you remember that San Diego nightclub? Well, the gorgeous ladies weren't dancing here either; I asked them all as a gentleman should. Consequently, I had the dance floor all to myself. I took off with leaps, turns and kicks, and danced until the set was over. After a zestful dance to fit the vibrant music, I was sweating profusely, but what a feeling!

Regretfully, after the dance, I only found frowns and stern faces in the place, not a smile to be seen anywhere. I am not a drinking man, and that can prompt uneasy feelings in bartenders. While paying for my sole beer, I think I saw the hint of a simper in the young barmaid's lips, but that was as far as she would go to answer my smile. So I just finished my beer and took off; perhaps it was a "Locals Only" club.

o o o

The House of the Rising Sun, by The Animals, was one of the biggest hits of the '60s. And there is really a house in New Orleans called The House of the Rising Sun, which is surrounded by legend and controversy.

Some say it was a brothel at 826 Saint Louis Street run by a Madame named LeSoleil Levant (Rising Sun), and that it brought ruin to many a good man. Others say the song refers to someone who sold his soul to the devil in that house, and is warning others to shun the deal.

But while sauntering down the French Quarter one day, looking for a place to play my drum for tips, I overheard a conversation. A coachman, driving his carriage alongside me, was telling his customers that the real House of the Rising Sun (he was pointing to it), had been owned by a French slave owner who had been extremely cruel to his slaves. His aberrant behavior and dissolute parties, which lasted until sunrise, made the rogue house famous.

And I do know that tourist guides can blatantly lie to their customers, without batting an eye or scratching their heads. But who knows? It could have been true. You figure it out.

I did not visit The House of the Rising Sun, but I was invited by a hostel employee to a voodoo ritual one night, where I found a motley crew of intriguing characters. The event was held outdoors, in the backyard of a house. I remember that when I first arrived, I was standing close to a high wooden fence, and a hard object hit my left arm.

For a moment, as I winced in pain, I thought that we were being attacked as part of the ritual, but we were not. The neighborhood kids were pelting us with stones, a gentleman told me. He went out and took care of the problem.

I think he was the same gentleman who escorted me out when I was leaving; he explained that the hoodlums in the neighborhood would do me in if I ventured outside alone. As we walked to my car, he pointed out their menacing shapes lurking in the dark, but they knew better than to mess with him.

He told me that he was the husband of the voodoo priestess who had been conducting the wedding ritual. I do not know if the wedding really took place, or if it was staged to get possessed, for as the ritual progressed, I could tell that they were indeed getting possessed.

What I remember of the ceremony was a young white man begging for the hand of a young black woman. In a rich, deep voice he would repeatedly declare his love and expound his virtues in crescendo, as the beautiful young lady rebuffed him in fashion.

The man vigorously twirled and contorted his body, repeating his request, while apparently invoking the spirits to his help. He ended his strenuous courting, kneeling on the ground, drenched in sweat, and possessed by a spirit or many. Sure that they were dealing with inorganic beings of some sort, I thought about asking the priestess before leaving, but she was extremely popular and therefore busy.

o o o

In a *gazing* meditation one morning, the scene in front of me turned into points of light, everything was light. *Seeing energy directly* is another of Castaneda's practices. You *see* the energy that forms the universe as you develop more presence through the practice.

Although I found Castaneda's version of *seeing energy directly* rather murky, later on, I found the practice explained by HH Rangjung Rigpe Dorje in a Buddhist text: "When the door of the mind, through which appearances are created, remains unobstructed, unwarped by concepts, then there is no solid reality, just bright light, and we let everything that appears just arrive naturally. Such a practice is the meditation of Mahamudra."

I wonder if voodoo priests *see* energy directly.

o o o

My trip to Florida started with the nagging feeling that I was heading in the wrong direction, perhaps a foreboding of what was to come. In Mississippi I felt like turning back. But I figured that if something wasn't of my liking, I could always return; I had to check it out. Stubborn!

o o o

I arrived at the Clearwater hostel around the end of July of 2003. And after systematically trying all the flea markets in the area from Webster to Tampa, I concluded that I had been doing much better in Texas. To tell you the truth, in Florida I was not making any money at all.

Other vendors told me, however, that the tourist season started around November, and sales would be excellent until April. Then, they explained, I would be able to recover and make a good profit. My stuff, they assured me, would sell well during the holidays, especially in Webster. I believed them. Why not?

Thus, I crossed the point of no return; I took advantage of a special promotion one of the companies I bought from had, to order enough merchandise for the season. My fate was sealed. That decision would plunge me into abject poverty; I was destined to face the four hurricanes that devastated Florida in 2004.

So, although I was lucky and missed Katrina, the hurricane that literally destroyed New Orleans, the other four obliterated my budding business, my savings turned into debt, and I ended losing everything I had, including the web store.

Incredibly, it has turned out to be a truly rewarding and interesting venture in many ways.

"When the heart weeps for what it has lost, the Spirit laughs for what it has found"—Sufi saying

o o o

While waiting for the tourist season to start, and before the aforementioned events happened, I did try the intentional community that was located in the area. I found them around the end of August of 2003.

It was late in the afternoon of a gray day with continuos rain in all its forms, when I found them near Plant City. The Chamber of Commerce gave me accurate directions to the rutted dirt road leading to my destination; the road took me straight to the farm. I parked close to the house.

After climbing out of my car and taking a few steps toward the building, I saw a man working in the field a short distance away; he was digging a hole. The terrain between us was a muddy quagmire, so I decided to go back to my car and change my footgear.

But when rushing back to the car, I saw someone exiting the house through the back door. The man was heading toward a barn located across a grassy field. I waved and called. He heard me, and decided that maybe I was worth a little time.

As he came nearer, I saw an unkempt beard and grizzled long hair tied back in a ponytail. His greeting was rather unfriendly, maybe because it was drizzling.

"What do you want?" he said dryly, looking at me askance.

I explained that I had come to see the farm, for I was interested in joining their budding intentional community. My statement seemed to put him on the defensive, perhaps because my visit had no previous notice. After he mentioned the fact, I explained having sent an email for which I never received an answer. He then called someone in the house and the man working in the field.

The young man arrived first. His hair was in dreadlocks and he wore glasses. He was stripped to the waist flaunting pierced, ringed nipples and an athletic built; with a pleasant smile, he introduced himself as Brian. An attractive woman with long grizzled hair joined us from the house. The older man introduced himself as Joshua and his wife as Jenny. He then said bitterly:

"This is Eco Farm!"

It was evident that something was amiss in Eco Farm, but I had nowhere to go in particular; and I had to wait for the tourist season to start, so I thought that perhaps I could help them. Joshua explained the purpose of my visit and they ushered me into the warm house.

Joshua had to go to the workshop to check something or other, so Brian and I sat at the living room table while Jenny worked in the kitchen; at times, she glanced suspiciously at me. Brian noticed the copy of the *Dhammapada* I was carrying, and he said that he was interested in Buddhism and meditation. That's when I thought that there was hope for the community.

Joshua returned and joined us at the table. I told them why I left Arcosanti. They gossiped about Rob, a disgruntled former resident that left Eco Farm, leaving all his belongings behind. They discussed the fact that he was a personable guy but not a community person; he would stay in his lodgings most of the time, reading.

Soon it was dinner time and I accepted their invitation. They were vegetarians, but that was fine with me; I was ravenous.

After a delicious dinner, we chatted in the living room; we planned a community with a link to the Source. I could tell that, although they disliked the fact that I was not young, they were beginning to trust me—even Jenny. They agreed to let me stay for a probation period of three weeks, as was their rule.

After three weeks, I had to leave for a three day evaluation. During those three days, we would assess our relationship and decide what my fate would be. That explained, Jenny ushered me to the guest room, so that I could take a shower while they had their weekly meeting.

The house was spacious: Counting the new ample guest room, it had three rooms, three bathrooms, a back porch leading to the kitchen, a front porch leading to the living room, and a larger kitchen was a work in progress.

I was exhausted, so after showering I went to bed.

That very night, I discovered that the train goes right through the house (or so it seemed), at about three o'clock in the morning. And in due course, I found out that even if you get used to it, and regardless of how tired you are, it shall wake you up.

The next morning we were up at dawn. Everyone had breakfast on his own as was the custom. Brian showed me where everything was; they had cereal, yogurt, soy milk, carob powder and wholesome multigrain bread. After breakfast, Brian fed Wolf, our German shepherd, (she got to be my best friend there to Brian's chagrin) and the elusive cat, and we headed to the orchards.

I remember that first day as busy. It was also hot and extremely humid; just an easy walk to the work location caused profuse sweating. We weeded; we removed scores of morning glory vines that were invading and smothering the ornamental trees; we worked around the many spiders living in their foliage.

Soon my clothes were drenched, as if I had taken a shower in them. I don't remember ever sweating like that, although I am sure I had.

o o o

The first couple of days everything went well, but I soon noticed inadequate communication; Joshua didn't talk much, specially in the mornings; he seemed upset, as if he'd rather be alone. Since he wouldn't talk, I never knew exactly what was expected of me. Before long, his dark mood had engulfed him throughout the day.

Brian had worked in the property for a while, so he knew what to do, but he wasn't much help either. They both had an uncanny ability to disappear in the mornings, or while working.

I had promised them that I would be upfront. So, after my second week, I confronted Joshua during our weekly meeting:

"I wanna talk to you."

"'bout what?" asked Joshua, in a rather hostile manner, as if he had been expecting a reaction from me.

"You're not talking. You've been acting as if you don't care to form a community."

"I don't," he blurted spontaneously. Then, realizing what he had just said, he tried to rectify and defend himself, eventually admitting his negative attitude and apologizing.

"I served in Viet Nam," he concluded, "sometimes my experiences there still affect me. Sorry 'bout that. Don't take offense."

Probably his past war experiences were really bothering him, but I could also tell that his ego played a big part in the drama. During my first week, I was able to organize a meditation session, which Jenny found enjoyable and helpful. Joshua was resentful, and subtly discouraged any more sessions. He was against the very thing that could have helped him the most.

Early one afternoon, I thought I was getting through to him about the importance of mindfulness. But apparently, his ego felt threatened whenever he was not in control of whatever was happening, and it wouldn't let him listen.

After our meeting, however, I thought he was making an effort to improve. For a couple of days, he even smiled in the mornings. When the probation period ended, we had another meeting in which it was decided that I should leave for three days, as we had agreed upon.

I went back to Clearwater, where I decided to sleep in my car to save money; at the ranch, I had worked for just room and board, and I had no other income. I used the ocean and the showers at the beaches to perform my ablutions. During my absence, I concluded that I could still help to form the community, for Joshua's attitude seemed to be improving. So during the third day of my exile, I called them, and they invited me to come back to discuss the matter.

o   o   o

Upon my return, we had a long discussion, exchanging thoughts and ideas that would perhaps improve our life in community. I tried to transmit the idea that no community could operate well, and prosper, without a good link to the Spirit; it is a necessity to see that our Source does not stand apart. After this meeting things went well for a few days. We drummed in the evenings almost every day; it was a meditation. Then Joshua started acting up again.

It happened a day in which we were moving heavy saplings to an area closer to the house. We were making a display next to the greenhouse, where they would stand out.

It was heavy, trying work: After we uprooted and carried the saplings to the new location, we had to dig holes to plant them. While at work, Joshua started making snide remarks about my shoveling, comparing it to the way Rob, the former member, used to shovel. Brian, being more a punk than a man, started following suit.

There was a time in my life in which such taunting behavior would have turned me into a cold, ruthless and vengeful individual, who would have spoken in a way that would undoubtedly have caused unforgivable violence. That *I* however, was dead now. Struck by inspiration, I just looked at them and recited a verse from the Diamond Sutra:

> "Regard this fleeting world
> As a star at dawn, a bubble in a stream
> A flash of lightning in a summer cloud,
> A flickering lamp, a phantom and a dream."

By the time I got to the third line they both had shut their mouths, and I didn't hear them again.

Still, an incident that occurred shortly after, helped me to understand that Eco Farm would never be a community: The new kitchen-in-progress needed a floor, and Joshua had hired David, a friend and neighbor, to do the job. The day David started working, I returned from the field early to find him looking perplexed and chagrined. David was a frequent visitor, and sometimes he joined us for dinner and beer, so I asked him what was wrong. He explained that no matter how he approached Joshua, he wouldn't listen.

The tiles had to be fitted on even ground. Joshua had put a layer of tar paper on the ground with the idea of preventing humidity from seeping through, and the tar paper was interfering with the proceedings. David knew that the job couldn't be done well if the tar paper wasn't removed, for the tiles couldn't be placed properly and they would soon crack.

Joshua was adamant. Jenny knew that David was experienced in his line of work, and she said that she had also tried to persuade Joshua to no avail; he wouldn't budge. As we were pondering David's problem, Joshua arrived. And as I started pleading with him to consider our friend's position David interrupted me:

"If the tar paper is not removed, it'll be a shitty job. I can't do it."

Joshua lost his temper.

"You can't do it?" he roared. "Then leave! Get out! I'll do it myself."

In silence, David grabbed his tools and left. Jenny and I also left the room. Joshua stayed working by himself until Brian came in to help him finish his fumble. It was obvious then that there was no point in staying in Eco Farm.

Where was the *community*? There could be no community where nobody but him had a saying; this was his ranch, his house and his kitchen, period! The next morning, I called a meeting to give notice. I told them that I would be ready to leave the following week.

A couple of days later, the floor started popping, like popcorn. You couldn't walk on the new floor because the tiles would crack. Joshua was (or is) a clear example of what the ego can do to a man.

When I left Eco Farm, he was in the process of redoing the floor, having wasted a few hundred dollars. Nonetheless, I could tell by the way he talked that he hadn't learned his lesson; his ego was still at the helm. I knew then, without a shadow of a doubt, why Rob had left in disgust, leaving his belongings behind.

Thus, after about a month of trying, I left Eco Farm. "Do not throw pearls to the pigs for they will trample on them."— the Christ

o o o

Is it true that a region can affect people? Can the energy of an area be detrimental to its inhabitants? Don Juan always had Castaneda scan the area in front of him, before choosing a place to rest, to avoid harmful locations. It was done by focusing on the area with your eyes partly closed, without looking directly at any place in particular, and waiting for a distinct feeling to guide you.

But even after I scanned an area to find a place to collect my thoughts and meditate, I still felt uneasy in Eco Farm. Arcosanti and the Sycamore Ranch were energizing places regardless of who was in them; Eco Farm was not. There was an undefinable, pervasive and diminishing influence within the site that I couldn't fathom, an eeriness that I couldn't comprehend. Was it the area itself? Was it the 3:00 AM train? Was it Joshua's ego oozing from everything?

Still, if by chance you find Eco Farm's website, it will show you beautiful pictures of an idyllic farm where you can join a sustainable, alluring *Intentional Community*. Aren't we masters of deceit?

It was the first week in October of 2003 when I left what I now call "Ego Farm: A Sweatshop" and business was still crawling. I was practically living in the flea markets, so I wouldn't have to pay rent; I couldn't afford it. My venture was about to fail altogether.

o o o

The flea market vendor experience varies from place to place, but it usually starts by searching for your stall in the darkness before dawn; and establishing in what direction you are facing, so that you can correctly set up your tables, or your tarp, amid the clanking of metal and the shafts of light shooting from restless flashlights. It is a rowdy atmosphere at times, with howls and cheers of anticipation, and a willingness to defy the weather with hot coffee, plastic coverings, blankets and persistence. It is a hardy lot.

I was always first in line because I slept in line. I would go to Webster on Mondays, Wesley Chapel on Tuesdays and Thursdays, and to Plant City on Wednesdays. I took Fridays off, stayed at the hostel, and shared a beer with my English friends, J___ and T___, travelers who were trying to stay in America. Saturdays and Sundays I worked the Wagon Wheel in Pinellas Park.

My next door neighbors at the Wagon Wheel recommended moving to the Mustang Flea Market next door. The Mustang was uncovered but my neighbors were right; I started to do a little better. By the end of October I was making my expenses. And all through the tourist season (November through April) that was all I made—my expenses.

Thus, I arrived at Florida's Tampa Bay the summer of 2003, and by the end of December of 2004 I was out of business. I did my best, but after weathering the four hurricanes brought by the summer heat, everyone in the area was picking up the pieces and rebuilding, and the tourists were avoiding Florida. Therefore, during the season, sales went down by around 60% and I couldn't take the loss. My business was gone.

I had taken a position as an independent contractor, taking signatures for petitions to put issues on the ballot for the following elections. Since I was not paying rent, that gig helped me pay some of my bills, but it didn't last long. And my old colt had to be put to rest; there was no choice. That little car had almost 250,000 miles on it.

So I had to take a loan to buy a newer car, and live from the remainder until I could start making a living again. The Powers That Be were giving me a chance to put my equanimity and inner balance to the test. Don't we all get those chances?

It really was a push forward; I had no choice but to live in mindfulness, while keeping in mind the old Haiku verse of a renowned Zen master:

> "The roof burnt down.
> That is good.
> I can see the moon."

Eventually, I returned to California and joined America's workforce again. So it was.

o o o

I did try to find a sangha,* but organized religion is such an easy prey for the ego that I had to stay on my own. I had similar results in New Orleans and San Diego, pompous and presumptuous individuals doing business with *Spirituality.* Chogyam Trungpa, a Buddhist meditation master, said that there are side roads, leading to versions of spirituality in which we merely strengthen our ego through spiritual techniques, what he calls spiritual materialism in his book *Cutting through Spiritual Materialism.*

At the sangha I approached in San Diego, I was trying to point out that methods imply time and disregard presence. I remember asking the Zen master a challenging question on the subject and he getting upset. His wife understood what I was trying to say but he was adamant. Haughtily, he asked me if I was enlightened.

So I told him that *I* couldn't be enlightened, because *I* was the problem. Although this is the core of the Buddha's teachings he was still inflexible; he asked me to keep silent in the meetings until I learned his *method.* Since I didn't really want to cause any strife, I just said, "Yes sir." But I saw the mark of *Spiritual Materialism*; I never went back.

Maybe by now, he has realized that enlightenment is something that we all have; we realize it as soon as we drop the *I,* as soon as we stop thinking and explaining to just *see* it. To just *see* that enlightenment has nothing to do with having anything (not even enlightenment), but with being aware that we are part of the Whole, and what we call *I* only exists as an ephemeral point of reference in a *dream.*

o o o

While I was still living at the hostel in Clearwater, I joined a health club, so that I could rehearse in the aerobics room and keep in shape. I was also hired by a cultural center to teach dance, but the class never developed. And since dancers are so self-centered, I was considering quitting dance altogether; it is

---

* Sangha, the Buddhist community of monks, nuns, novices, and laity; in this case, a group to meditate with.

a performing art after all, and the ego thrives in the performing arts, doesn't it?

But one day that I was in a Barnes and Noble bookstore, I found a book about Tibetan Buddhist monks who danced.

"I'll be damned," I muttered.

I picked up the book and there they were: elaborate dances with striking costumes, magnificent leaps, graceful postures, and apparently, no ego. I read on.

The author said that when they perform in America, all you see is performance and style, technique and form, but no self-aggrandizement, no self-importance. The dancers say that the choreography comes from Beyond, from the Mother of all Buddhas. I believed them. I decided to keep dancing.

Dance for the Spirit of humanity. Dance for the sake of dance.

Chapter 13

The Woman in the Park

More boldly, I would say that our very presentness is our salvation;
the present moment entered into fully, is our gateway to eternal life.
                                                        —Phillip Simmons.

We must not wish anything other than what happens from moment
to moment.   *—St Catherine of Genoa*

There is a common belief, which appears in all civilizations
throughout time; what Aldous Huxley calls *The Perennial Phi-*
losophy. It refers to "an infinite, timeless Reality beyond the
world of the senses that, although not manifest, lies at the core
of everything that exists."

For sentient beings, the intrinsic challenge in life is to experience this Reality while we are still alive, to experience our
totality—to *awake* in dreamless sleep. All the great teachers
agree upon the fact that to accomplish this feat, we have to conquer the enemy within, the ego: A false "self" that feeds on our
constant preoccupation with an unalterable past, imaginary
situations and a nonexistent future. The most devastating effect
of our mental menagerie is the concealment of our link to the
Spirit. All the roads I have found intersect at one point: presence.

In the last few months I have come to fully cement the realization that the world of form is the reign of the ego because
there is no choice. For when there is form there is separation,

and the *I thought* has to form to identify everything else. The ego (mind) has to be there for us to be able to interact with the world; this is not the problem.

The ego, however, will not accept itself for what it is: the gatekeeper of a *dream*; it grabs the baton and declares itself real, and, one way or another, eternal. And here lies the problem: We identify ourselves with an impostor. We become the slaves of a *false* self who hides our link to our Source, to our boundlessness, and in our blindness we create hell; in our ignorance, we are even willing to die defending the impostor.

o o o

We use methods and equations to try to understand the meaning of everything, to try to solve the riddle of life, to figure out why we can't live in peace. But when we think we understand Reality with our intellect, we are as far away from it "as heaven is from earth." We are using the wrong tool for the job.

What the Buddha, the Christ and all sages throughout time have tried to teach us, is indeed very simple: Happiness is accessible right now to all those who are willing to do the work and subdue the ego. The Truth is right in front of us, but if we don't bypass the ego's dissertations, we will not *see* it.

Our challenge consists in living life in this world, which is so absorbing and full of traps, and at the same time attain awareness of the Absolute, which underlies it, attaining what Castaneda calls, the *totality of ourselves. Awakening* is the realization of that totality, the realization of the Absolute in the world of form, of the fact that all is the Mind Essence—the One.

Our challenge is to see that in silence there is *God*. Our challenge is to see that if we stop babbling to ourselves uselessly, we will see that the magic kingdom of heaven is spread upon the earth right *now*, but we are not *seeing* it. Our challenge is to *awake* and *see* that there is a depth to us that we weren't aware of.

Understanding the teachings of all masters past and present, I have realized, is of no help whatsoever unless we commit to practice mindfulness, unless we go to the gist of the matter and become selfless. If we don't apply what we know, we will be like the spoon in the soup: It is submerged in the soup but it can't taste it. Our knowledge will be useless. That is why Zen Buddhist monks disregard scriptures and go to the practice, for the degree of control of a wandering mind is the measure of progress in awakening.

o o o

It was while in Santa Barbara, CA when I *saw* clearly the human predicament. That day after work, I parked my car on Garden Street by the Alameda Park, the area where I *camped*. It was late in the afternoon of a magnificent sunny day; sun rays slanted among the trees bordering the walkways; somewhere, a mockingbird sang. I reclined the driver's seat back and relaxed.

After a short time, I noticed a woman crossing the park. She was tall and well dressed, probably coming home from work. She was walking in haste, immersed in self-reflection, looking down at the ground.

There was no one else in the park, and somehow, the solitary figure poignantly made me *see* the vulnerability of human beings when immersed in self-reflection. She was trapped in thought unaware of her surroundings. She was, I could tell, unaware of the present moment, which was slipping away like sand through her fingers.

I *saw* the trap of self-reflection. I *saw* the huge net that captures and enslaves the human race. Sadness engulfed me. I wasn't different. I was trapped myself.

And for years, late during sunny afternoons, the memory tugged at my heart on occasion. It doesn't anymore. Now the memory of the woman in the park is there only for reference; I am writing about it. Paradoxically, it will remain to remind me not to dwell in the past, or to feel sad, but to live and accept the present challenge of seeing life as it is *now*: a temporary magical show!

o o o

The eye of the dragon! I like the concept: Only by becoming invisible, and then nothing, can we pass through the eye of the dragon, avoiding its fiery jaws. But of course, there is no eye, no dragon, no gate; it's all a metaphor, for we are never separate from the Source. We just need to be aware of it. The eye of the dragon is right *here,* staring at you!

Can you *see* it?

Afterword

. . . One ring to bring them all and in the darkness bind them.
—The Lord of the Rings, JRR Tolkien

I had a disturbing vision recently. I *saw* a severed arm lying on the ground, and upon close examination, I *saw* bruises and swelling, and blood running down the length of the forearm. The sight was revolting and I withdrew.

At times, visions have a way to reflect the situation we find ourselves in, or our state of mind, and presently we have a state of constant war, which implies dismemberment in many ways. It also creates turmoil.

So that vision could have been related to evidence I came across recently. Evidence (found by a group of architects and engineers[*] on ground zero in New York City) proving that in September 11, 2001, the *three* World Trade Center buildings were brought down by controlled demolition. The implications are grave because the government has been not only denying the evidence, but apparently, also destroying it.

Has the ego spawned a monster in our midst?

o o o

Now more than ever we need to be aware of how the ego steers individuals and societies toward conflict and war; now

---

[*] www.AE911Truth.org

more than ever we need to change our *dream*. Our decisions, no matter how small, must be conscious decisions based on awareness.

We must be aware of what is occurring, and accept our own responsibility in the matter. We must be aware of who we really are, in order to *see* how everything is interconnected, and move toward peace instead of toward destruction, toward evolution instead of toward oblivion.

We have reached a crossroads.

Acknowledgments

I am indebted to Carlos Castaneda's work; his books opened for me doors to the unlimited potential in human beings. I am also indebted to my editors at Create Space, and to all the employees at the Apple store in Fashion Valley, San Diego, CA who taught me word processing, cover design and layout. Also to my friends Debbie Wing and Heather Blanco for their valuable comments.

And, of course, to all those who have crossed my path, for they have directed me *here*, one way or another.

Bibliography

Bancroft, Anne, Ed., *The Pocket Buddha Reader,* 2001
Buck, William, Trans. *The Mahabharata,* 2000
Easwaran, Eknath, Trans., *The Baghavad Gita,* 2007
Easwaran, Eknath, Trans. *The Upanishads,* 2007
Evans-Wentz, W. Y., Trans. *The Tibetan Book of the Dead,* 2000
Goddard, Dwight, Trans. *A Buddhist Bible,* 1994
Goodman, David, Ed., *Be as You Are: The Teachings of Sri R. Maharshi,* 1989
Gurdjieff, G.I., *Beelzebub's Tales to His Grandson,* 1950
Hagen, Steve, *Buddhism Is Not What You Think,* 2004
Huxley, Aldous, *The Perennial Philosophy,* 2009
Kapleau, Phillip, *The Three Pillars of Zen,* 1989
Krishnamurti, J., *Total Freedom: The Essential Krishnamurti,* 1996
Malone, Calvin, *Razor-Wire Dharma: A Buddhist Life in Prison, 2008*
Nagrin, Daniel, *How to Dance Forever,* 1988
Rinpoche, T. W., *The Tibetan Yogas of Dream and Sleep,* 1998
Ruiz, don Miguel, *The Four Agreements,* 1997
Smith & Novak, *Buddhism, A Concise Introduction,* 2004
Tagore, R., *Bhagat Kabir ji, Poems,* 1986
Tolkien, J.R.R., *The Lord of the Rings,* 1980
Warner, Brad, *Hard Core Zen,* 2003
Wright, M. S., *Behaving as if God in all Life Mattered,* 1997
Wikipedia
Yogananda, Paramahansa, *Autobiography of a Yogi,* 1946
Zondervan, *Holy Bible,* 1993

Made in the USA
Charleston, SC
14 May 2012